ABANDONED AND FORGOTTEN CEMETERIES OF PHILADELPHIA AND ITS ENVIRONS

ED SNYDER

AMERICA
THROUGH
TIME

America Through Time®
An imprint of Sutton Publishing Inc
www.through-time.com

First published 2025

ISBN 978-1-63499-523-8

Typeset in Trade Gothic 10pt on 15pt
Printed and bound in the United States of America by Integrated Books International

ACKNOWLEDGMENTS

The author would like to thank the following people for their gracious help in researching this book, a process that actually began in 2010 without him even realizing it:

Ted Adams
Stephen Anderer
Rachel Bailey
Michael Barnes
Scarlett Bat
Bill Caraker
Jo Cosgrove
Steve Finkelman
Sharon Haines
George Hofmann
Tom Keels
Faith B. Kuehn
Jill LeMin Lee
Mark Pugnetti
Jenn O'Donnell
Frank Rausch
Paulette Rhone
Ken Smith
Olivia Snyder
Neil Sukonik
Paul Wismar

CONTENTS

INTRODUCTION

Show me your cemeteries and I will tell you what kind of people you have.

Benjamin Franklin, *c.* 1736

In 2016, workers digging the foundation for a new condominium project in Philadelphia were greeted by the accidental exhumation of human skeletons. Within days, it was determined that the excavation was being conducted at the site of the graveyard of the First Baptist Church of Philadelphia (founded in 1698)—a graveyard whose contents were supposedly relocated to the city's Mount Moriah Cemetery in 1860. Hundreds of bodies in wooden coffins were excavated by archeologists over the next few days.

Some of Philadelphia's colonial-era resting places remain but most do not. Why? Cemeteries are business ventures. Even a church's private graveyard, such as that of the Old Swedes Church in Queen Village, has operating costs. This Episcopal church was founded in 1697, yet it keeps its graveyard maintained and active. When a cemetery can no longer turn a profit—or at least cover its costs—there is potential for failure. We will examine Philadelphia-area cemeteries that have fallen on hard times, properties that have not been able to provide the "perpetual care" that they promised their customers. We will also look at the many ways a cemetery can falter.

From its inception, the city grew exponentially, its population jumping from 81,000 in 1800 to over half a million people by the time of the Civil War. In the first 170 years of its existence, cemeteries large and small were established to bury the dead. By the 1860s, there was no land left to expand these burial grounds to accommodate future burial needs. The Civil War, of course, presented massive and unforeseen issues related to burying vast amounts of bodies quickly. Large rural cemeteries began to appear. Small inner-city cemeteries and church graveyards felt the pressure as property values grew. Some of these small graveyards were moved to rural locations. Some were just built over.

Historian Tom Keels describes three waves of cemetery destruction in Philadelphia, all to provide its inhabitants with space for housing, commerce, and recreation.[1] The first wave of cemetery removal occurred between 1865 and 1895 as the city grew highly industrial and building intensified. Between 1910 and 1926, church graveyards and neglected cemeteries were removed. Keels says that while removal of remains were supposed to be handled respectfully, political corruption and shoddy workmanship made the process less than ideal. After World War II, political pressure for urban renewal and expansion forced the replacement of many larger cemeteries with playgrounds, parking lots, and supermarkets.

The 2016 First Baptist Church example mentioned earlier is not the only recent cemetery surprise in Philadelphia. Shortly after digging began in 2010 to renovate south Philadelphia's Weccacoe Playground, 5,000 African American graves were discovered. While many Philadelphia cemetery stories make us really wonder what kind of people we are, some recent examples give us hope. In many cases, volunteers have prevented a particular cemetery's demise. Volunteer groups have gotten involved and worked toward the goal of stabilizing a faltering property, preserving and restoring it, and sometimes even turning it back into an active cemetery. Ben Franklin would have sung the praises of the many volunteers responsible for these selfless acts.

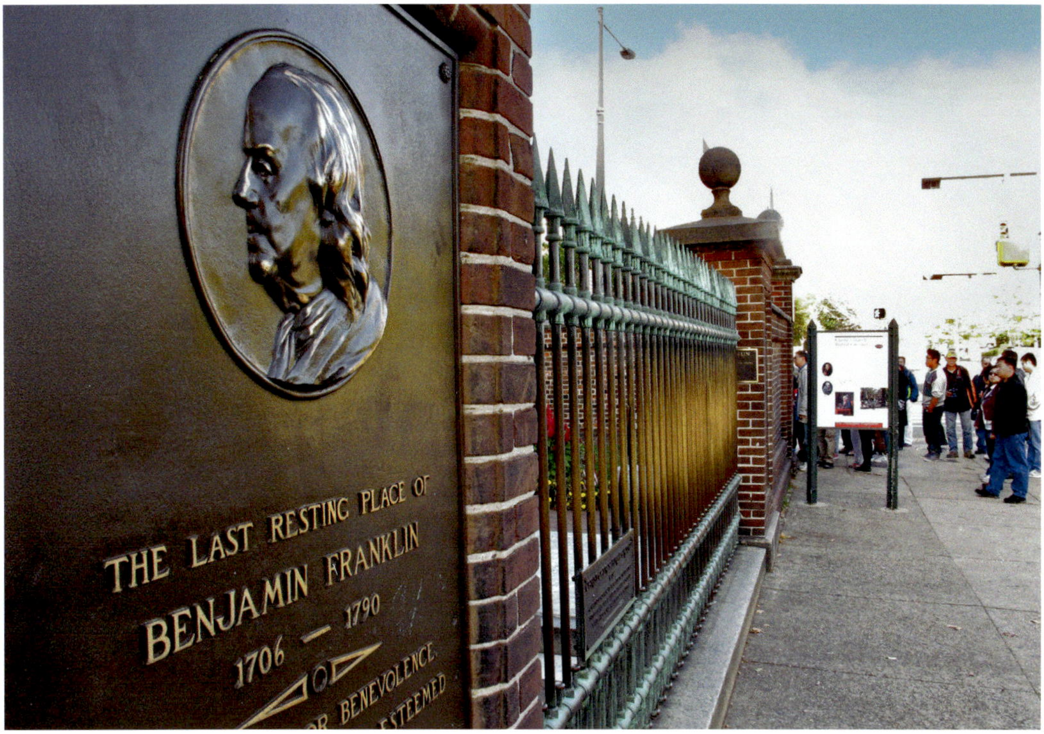

Ben Franklin's grave lies behind this wall at Christ Church Burial Ground in Philadelphia.

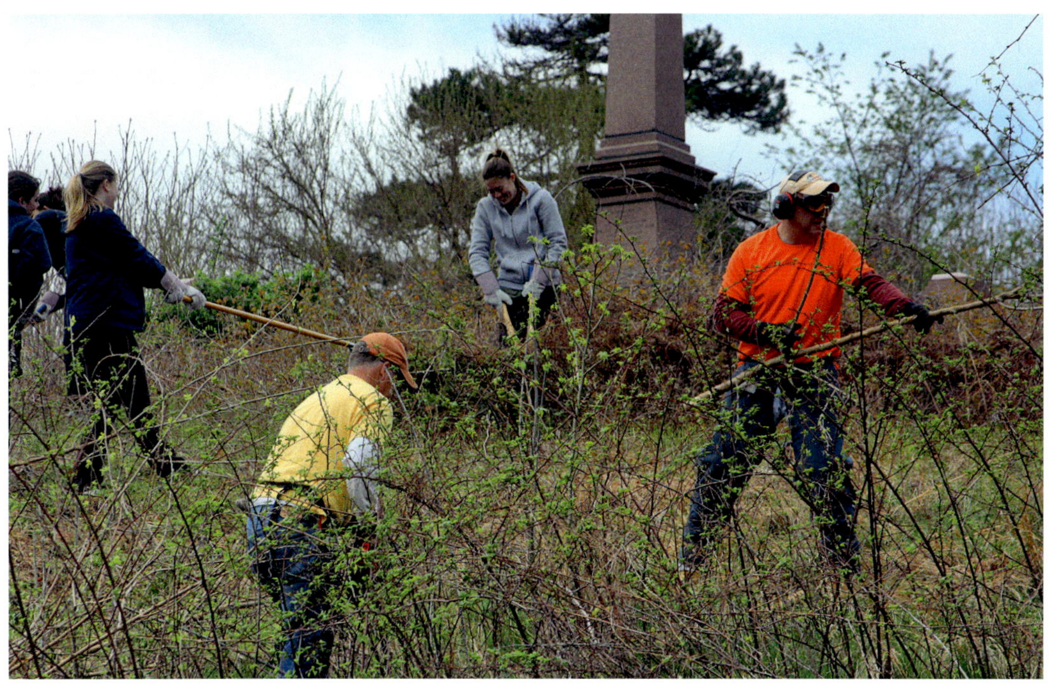

Volunteer cleanups sponsored by the civic engagement programs of various colleges and businesses continue from spring through fall at Philadelphia's Mount Moriah Cemetery. The Friends of Mount Moriah Cemetery, Inc. invite volunteers to visit their website at friendsofmountmoriahcemetery.org/volunteer.

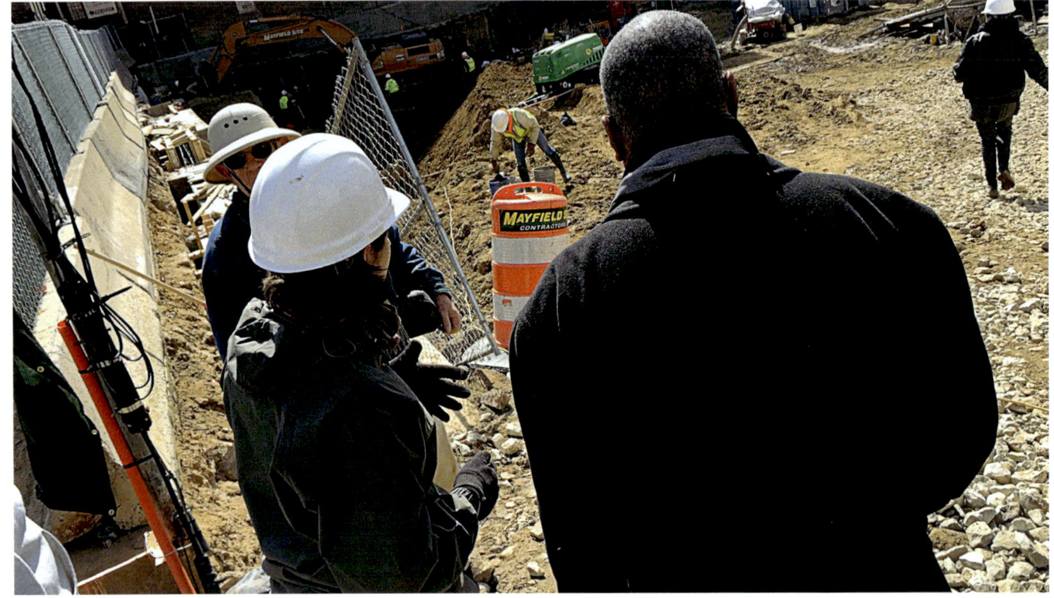

Archeologist speaks to press at Arch Street dig in 2017 where graves from First Baptist Church of Philadelphia were unearthed.

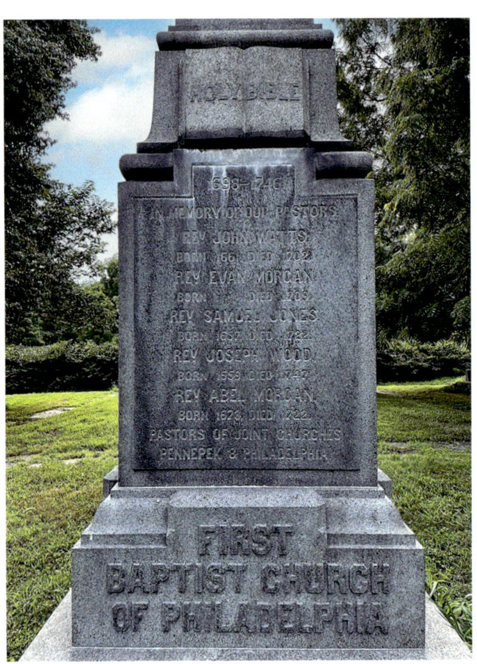

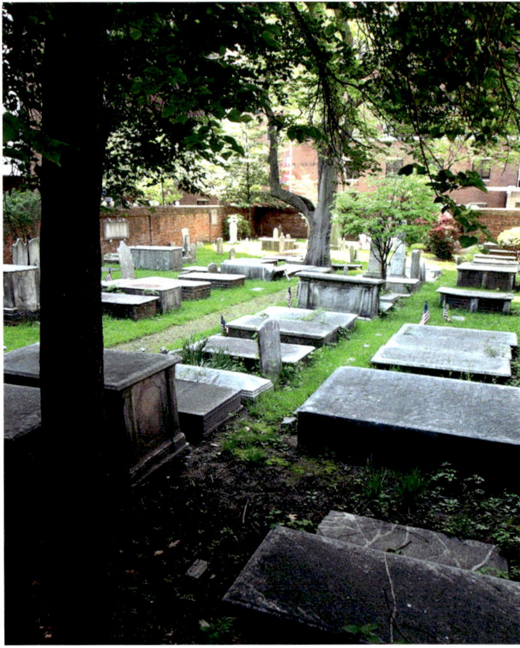

Above left: The First Baptist Church of Philadelphia purchased a large plot and monument in Mount Moriah Cemetery in 1860, for the purpose of relocating graves from its original Arch Street location.

Above right: Founded in 1740, Mikveh Israel Cemetery at Eighth and Spruce Streets is the oldest Jewish cemetery in Philadelphia. Nathan Levy, whose ship brought the Liberty Bell to America rests here, along with Rebecca Gratz, the model for Sir Walter Scott's heroine Rebecca in *Ivanhoe.*

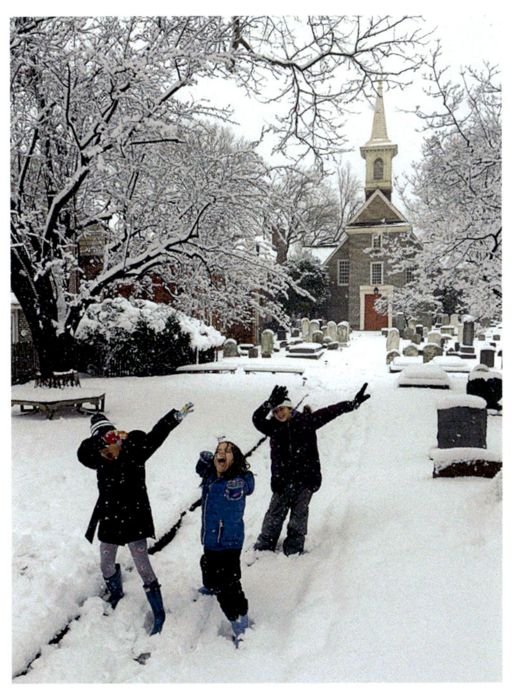

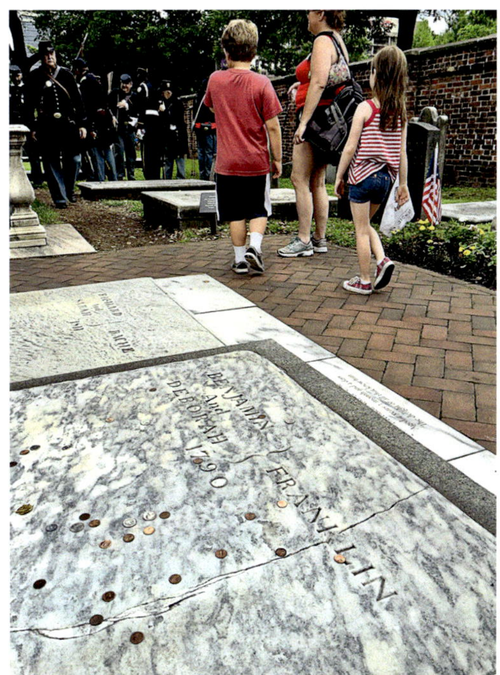

Above left: Neighborhood children frolic in the snow at Gloria Dei Old Swedes Church in Philadelphia's Queen Village neighborhood. Betsy Ross was married in the church in 1777, which was established in 1700. It is the oldest active congregation in the United States and its graveyard still accommodates new burials.

Above right: The grave of Ben and Deborah Franklin in Christ Church Burial Ground is a popular tourist destination in Philadelphia's historic district. The cemetery was established in 1719.

Right: An historic marker for the Bethel Burying ground was installed in 2019 at Weccacoe Playground, Fourth and Catharine Streets. One of the first independent cemeteries for free African Americans, the property was sold to the city after the church moved in 1889.

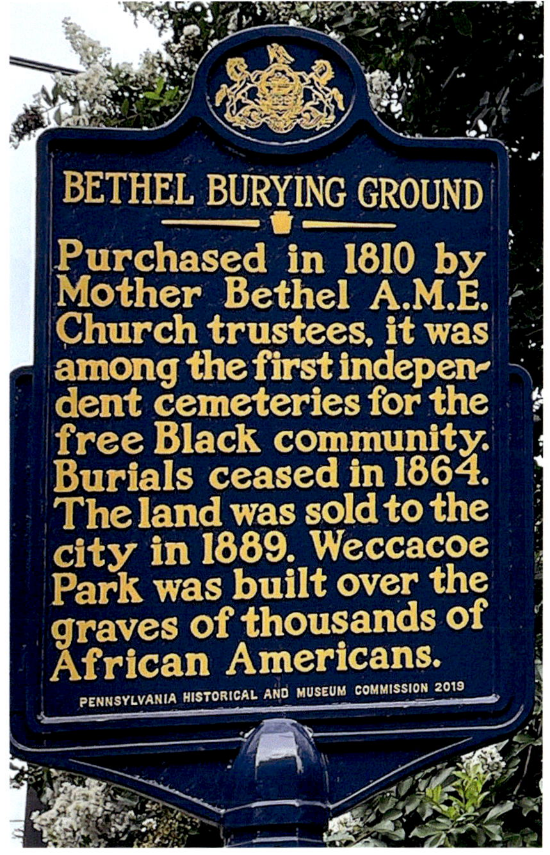

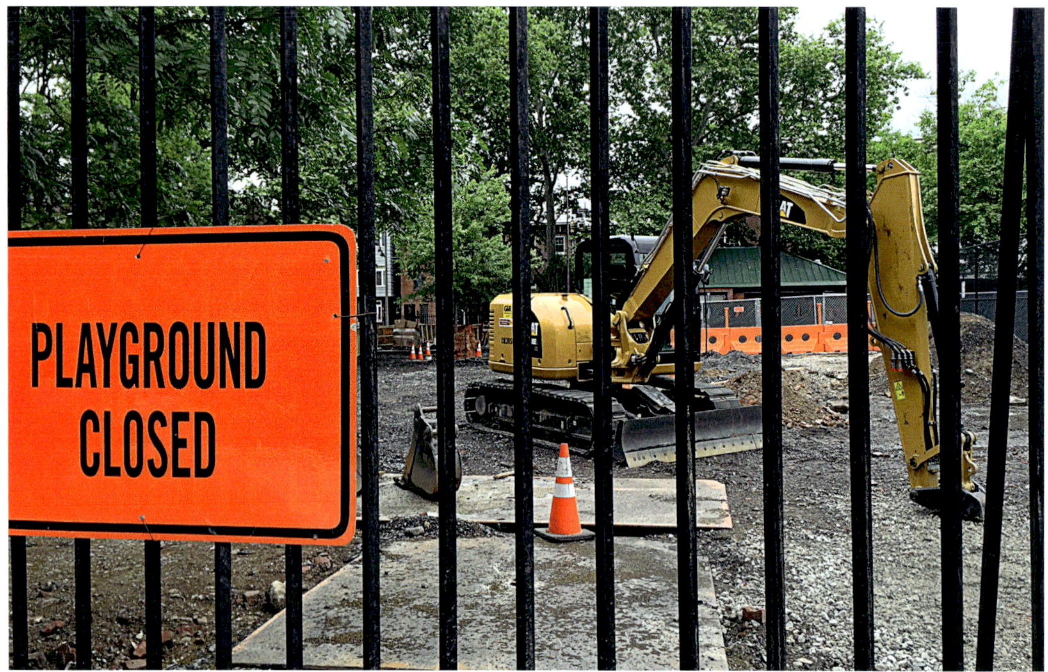

Construction was interrupted at south Philadelphia's Weccacoe Playground in 2013 when graves were unearthed during a park improvement project.

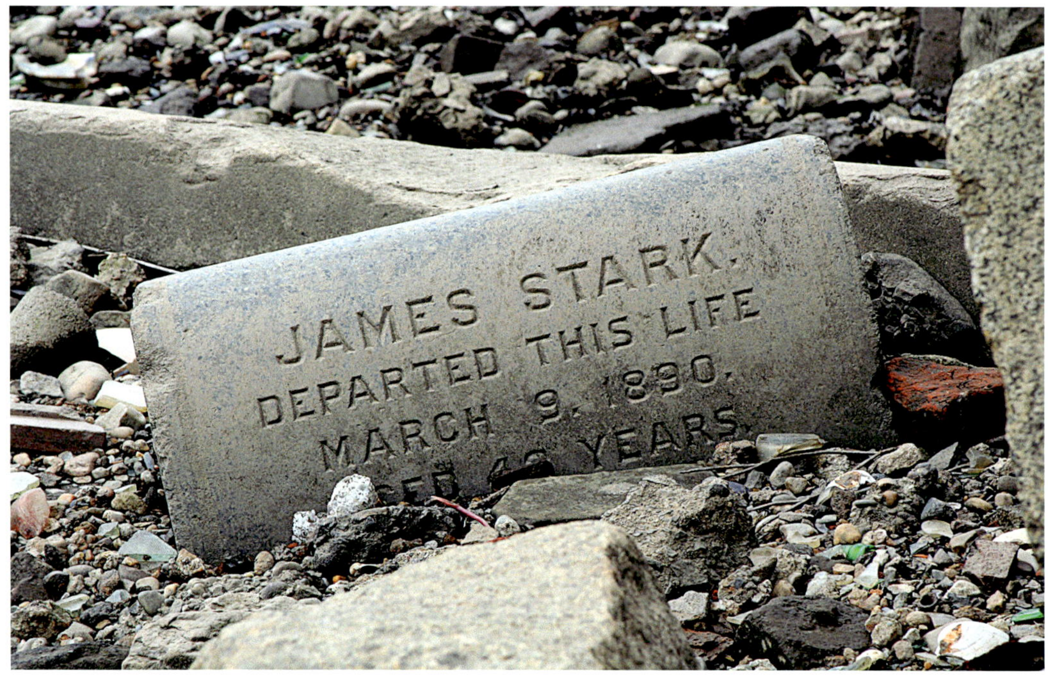

The names would be obscured until the next low tide, but because of current public interest in what happened to Monument Cemetery, their memory lives on in ways they never could have expected.

1

WHY AND HOW ARE CEMETERIES ABANDONED?

Chances are that the cemetery in your neighborhood will remain intact for your lifetime; however, the one in the next town may be washed away in a flood. While each disappeared cemetery is affected by unique circumstances, we can say that many become filled, cannot accommodate additional burials, and therefore cease to generate revenue. At that point, the owners are faced with tough decisions. Walking away is one option.

The fates of some cemeteries can be analyzed relative to the era in which they existed. San Francisco, for instance, banned all new burials within its city limits in 1901 and condemned all of its city cemeteries in 1912 for the sake of land development.[1, 2] The city was expanding, cemeteries were targeted, and tombstones and monuments were dumped into San Francisco Bay.[3]

There are other reasons cemeteries disappear. Religious congregations that own burial grounds have in many cases disbanded. The church building or synagogue is gone. This happened with B'nai Israel Cemetery in southwest Philadelphia. It was established in 1856 by a Dutch Jewish congregation, which disbanded in 1879. The cemetery was eventually abandoned.

Some cemeteries are still there, you just cannot see them. This is the case with south Philadelphia's Mother Bethel Burying Ground and Camden, New Jersey's Johnson Cemetery Park. The former is now Weccacoe playground. Across the Delaware River from Philadelphia, Camden reimagined a run down, historic 1854 African American Civil War Veterans' cemetery as a grassy park in the late 1970s.

Cemeteries can become derelict or abandoned abruptly, or over time. In the early part of the twentieth century, perpetual care endowments were a common funding source for grave maintenance (a percentage of the sale price of a grave goes toward the perpetual fund). However, with bank failures after the stock market crash in 1929, endowments and trust funds vanished. This was one reason Philadelphia's Laurel Hill Cemetery suffered.

Laurel Hill was the second rural garden cemetery established in America, in 1836. This followed the first, Mount Auburn Cemetery in Cambridge, Massachusetts, in 1831. Both were patterned after the original garden cemetery, Père Lachaise, Paris, established 1804. Laurel Hill found itself in a precarious situation in the 1970s. It was overcrowded with burials by 1900 and suffered a steady decline after World War II. Financial instability led to neglect, the declining neighborhood fostered vandalism and other crime. Many of the Tiffany stained-glass windows in mausoleums were stolen, monuments were covered with graffiti. A volunteer Friends group formed in 1978, the Friends of Laurel Hill Cemetery, which saved the magnificent sculpture garden. Today it thrives.

Not every cemetery has a savior. Philadelphia's push for urban renewal after World War II resulted in the obliteration of many burial places, both large and small. In some cases, graves were moved; in others, they were not. Mario Lanza Park had been the Trinity Episcopal Church graveyard. The William Dick public schoolyard had been the Odd Fellows Cemetery. The Southwark/Queen Village Community Garden was the Ebenezer Church Burial Ground. Palumbo Playground and recreation center had been the Ronaldson Cemetery. Union Burial Ground is now a strip mall parking lot. Perhaps most notoriously, Capitolo Playground had once been the large Lafayette Cemetery (see next chapter).

It is tempting to think that all this upheaval happened quietly, behind the scenes. But imagine your grandparents in 1922 going to visit graves in Philadelphia's Hanover Street Burial Ground. Imagine them seeing a sign posted at the fence that said: "The City of Philadelphia has taken over this property for a recreation center. All bodies must be promptly removed."[4] This was progress.

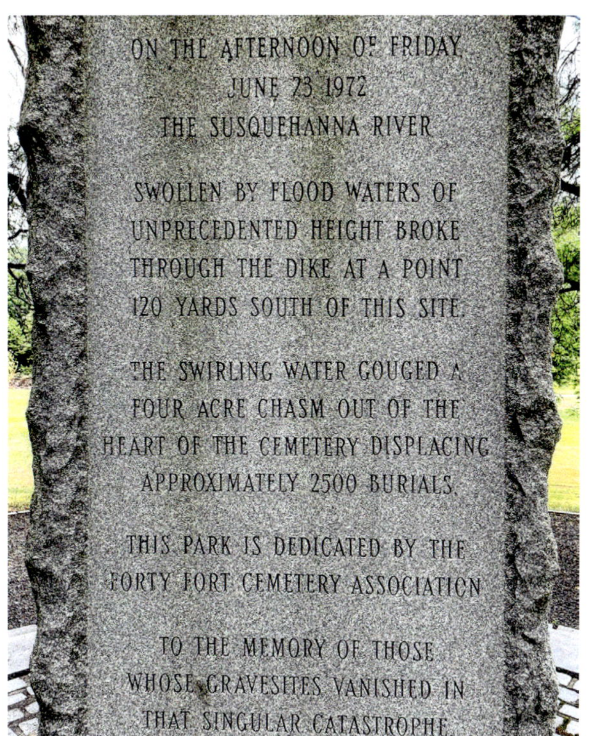

A monument was erected on the spot where in 1972, the Susquehanna River gouged the cemetery in Forty-Fort, Pennsylvania, and washed away 2,500 graves.

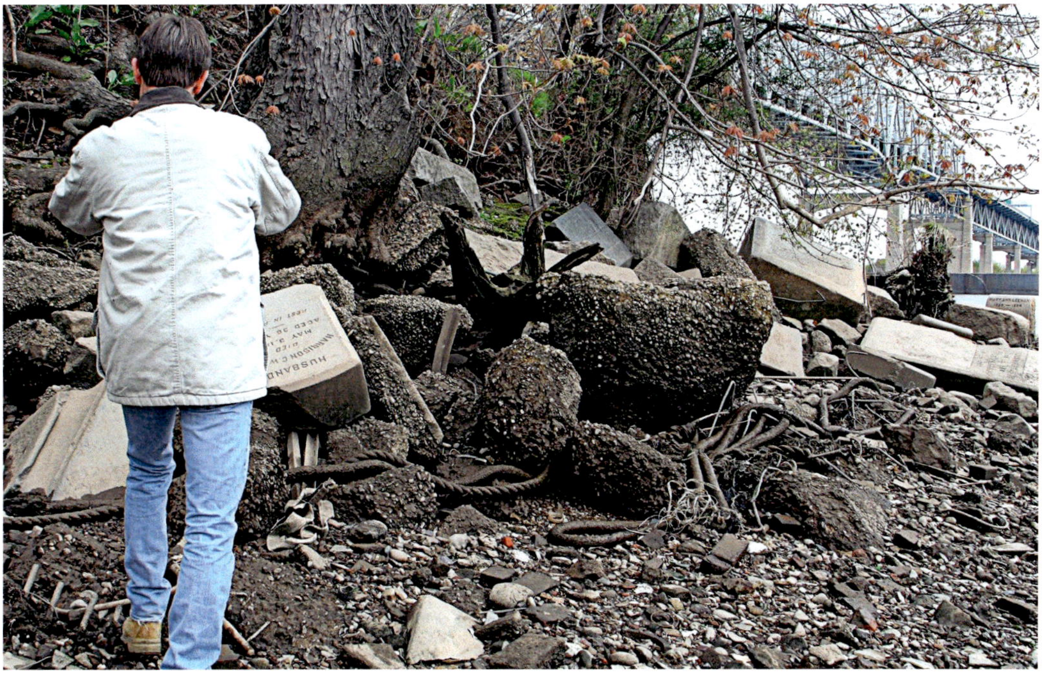

The Philadelphia riverfront under the Betsy Ross Bridge is littered with grave markers from Monument Cemetery. The cemetery on North Broad Street was dismantled in 1956 and the stones used to bolster the shoreline for the planned construction of the bridge.

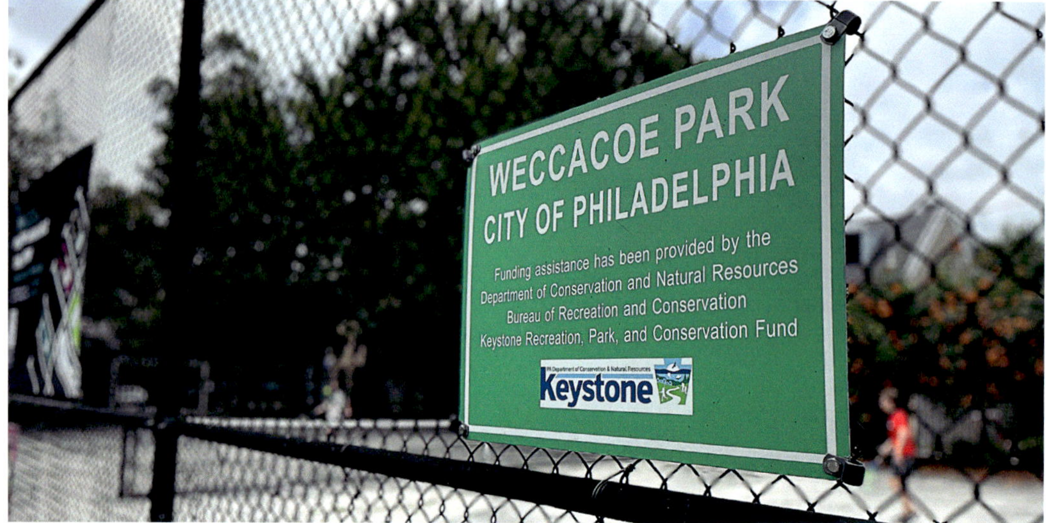

Below the tennis court and recreation center in Weccacoe Park lie 5,000 bodies. The Mother Bethel A.M.E. Church established its Bethel Burial Ground in 1810. The church moved away in 1889, selling the graveyard to the City of Philadelphia. By 1900, it had been transformed into a park, dubbed Weccacoe Square.

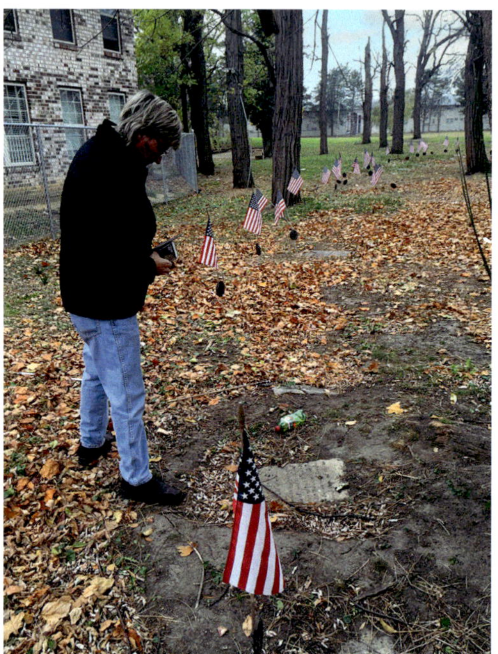

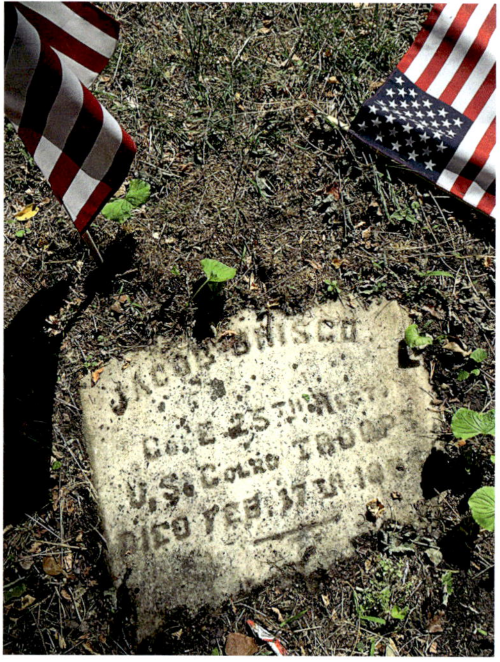

Johnson Cemetery Park in Camden, New Jersey, was essentially a grassy park prior to neighborhood cleanup volunteers accidentally uncovering the laid-flat grave markers in 2010. The 1854 African American cemetery was essentially laid to rest in the 1970s when 123 USCT veterans and others had their headstones either thrown into the Delaware River or laid flat as sidewalk pavers by the City of Camden.

Private Jacob Brisco of the 25th Regiment U.S. Colored Troops, Company E, served in the Union Army during the American Civil War. He mustered out on December 6, 1865, and died on February 17, 1886. His headstone in Johnson Cemetery in Camden is likely nowhere near his grave but lies with twenty others in an undignified manner as a sidewalk paver.

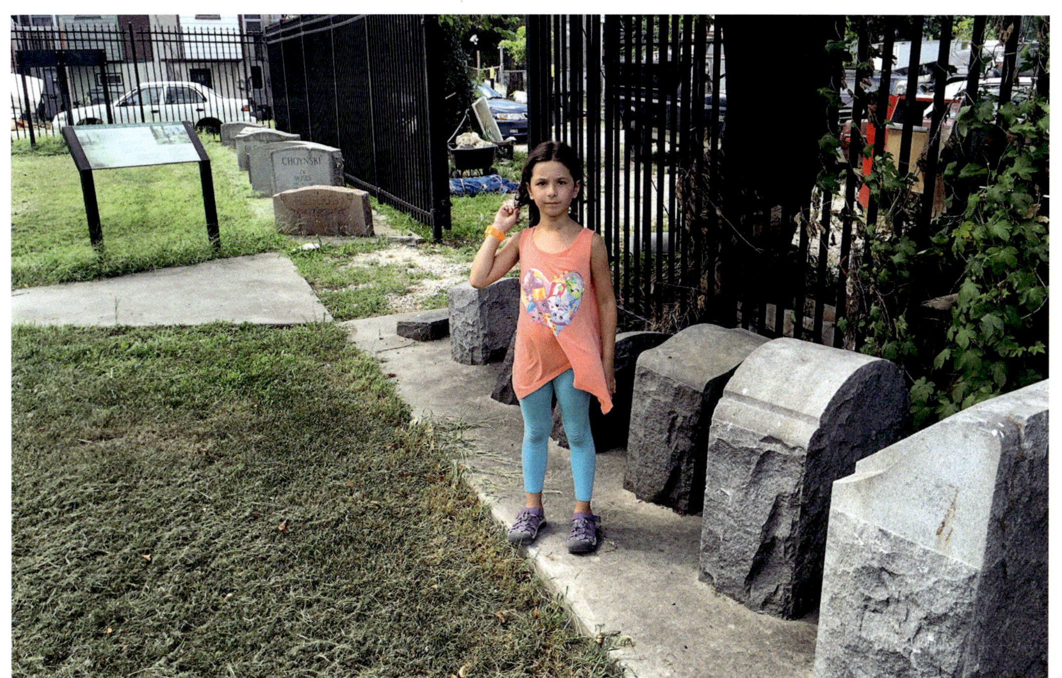

Above: B'nai Israel Cemetery near Sixty-Fifth Street and Chester Avenue was preserved in 1999 by setting the remaining whole grave markers in concrete around the perimeter of the property. Prior to that, the cemetery was filled with trash as well as the toppled and broken grave markers of 440 people (including Civil War veterans); it was listed by the city as an abandoned property.

Right: Mausoleum stained-glass windows have been targeted by thieves, especially vintage glass crafted by Tiffany Studios.

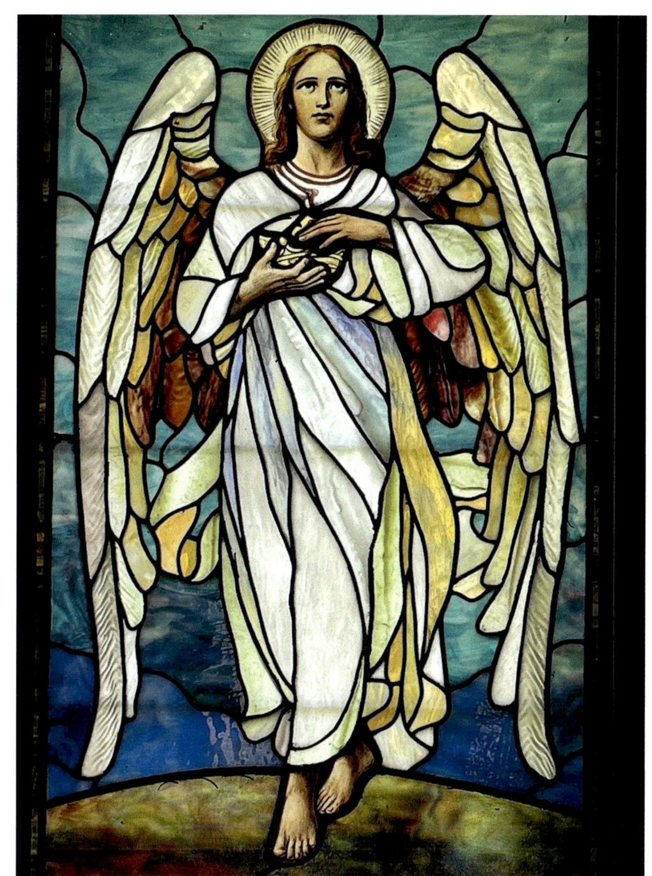

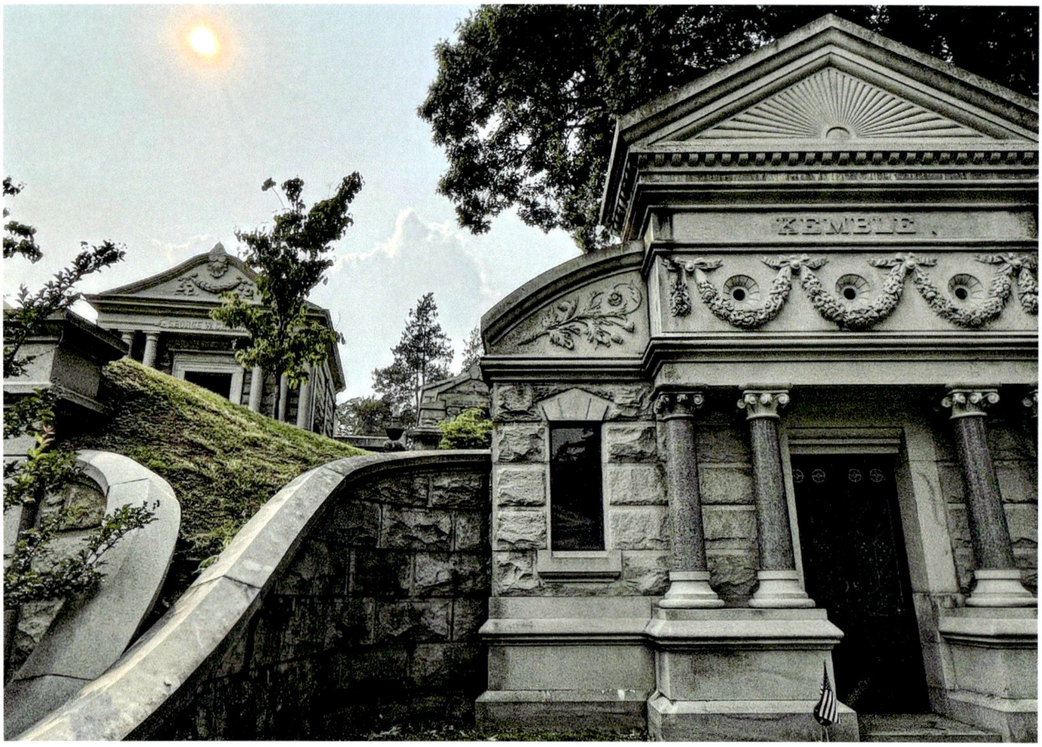

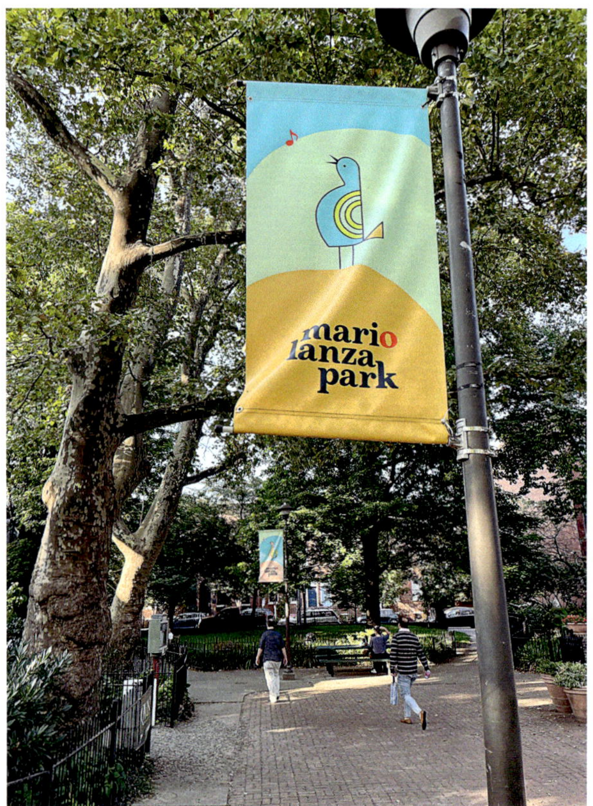

Above: Opulent mausoleums line "Mausoleum Row" in Philadelphia's Laurel Hill Cemetery, the nation's second Victorian rural cemetery.

Left: Mario Lanza Park is named for the American opera singer and actor (1921–1959) who was born a few blocks from the park. The Mario Lanza Park, at Second and Catharine Streets, had been the graveyard of Trinity Episcopal Church (est. 1820), until the church was closed in 1913. Some of the tombstones and remains were removed to Mount Moriah by 1919.

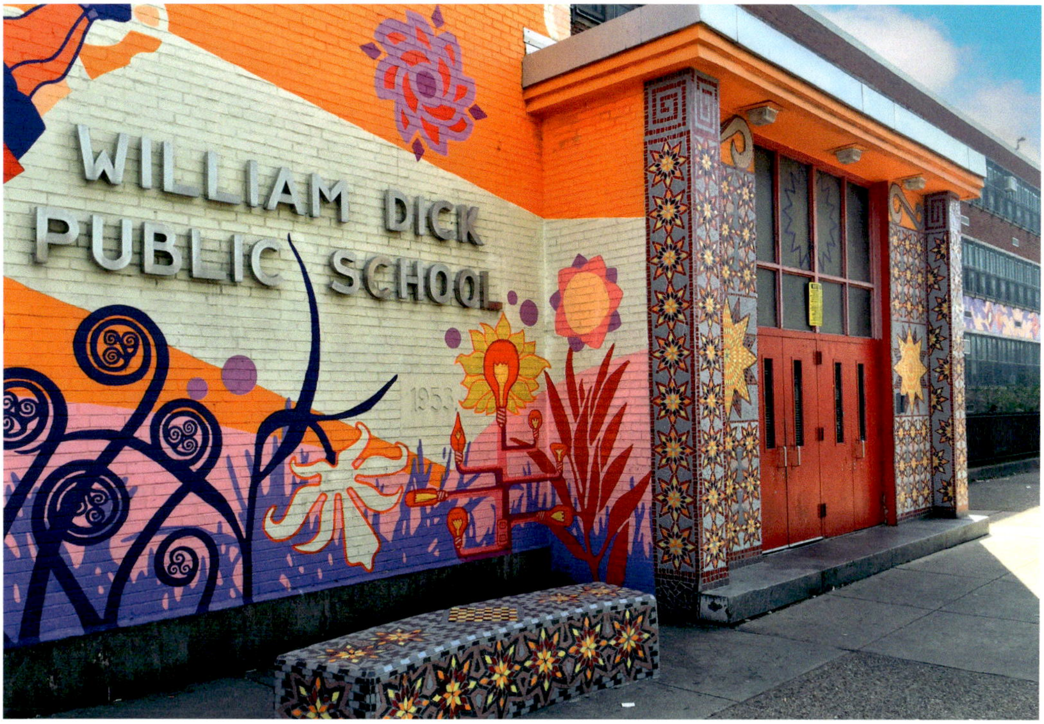

The William Dick School at Twenty-Fourth and Diamond Streets was built in 1951, on the site of the Odd Fellows Cemetery (est. 1849). About 80,000 bodies were supposedly moved for the project.

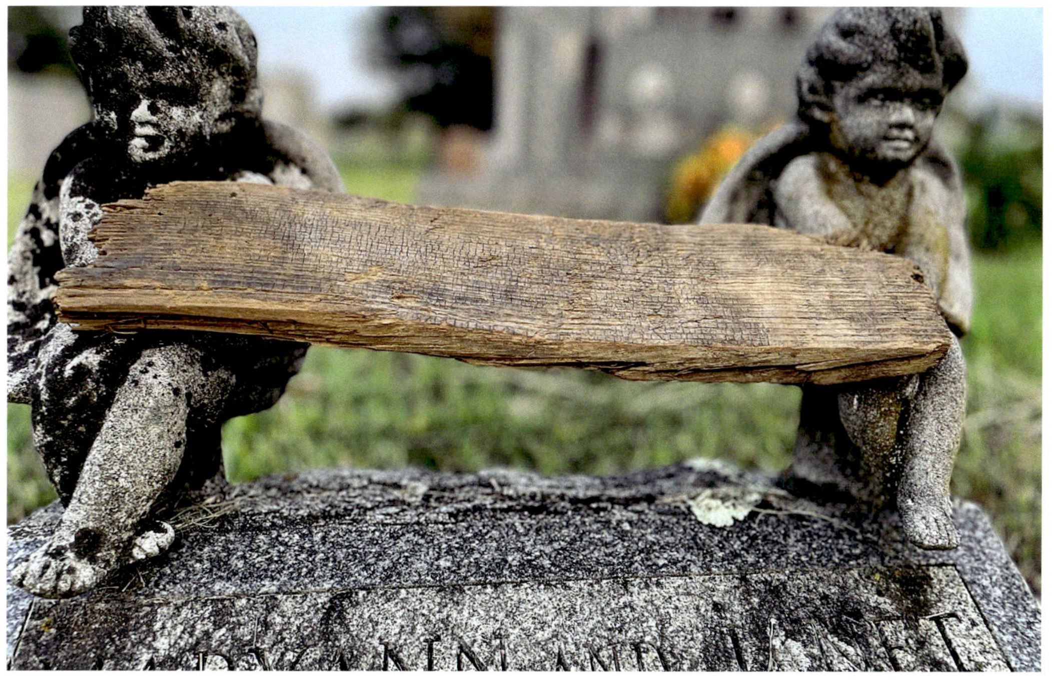

In 2013, six wooden coffins with skeletal remains were surprisingly unearthed by the Philadelphia Water Company under the schoolyard of the William Dick School. Photo shows piece of a pine box coffin unearthed at the site.

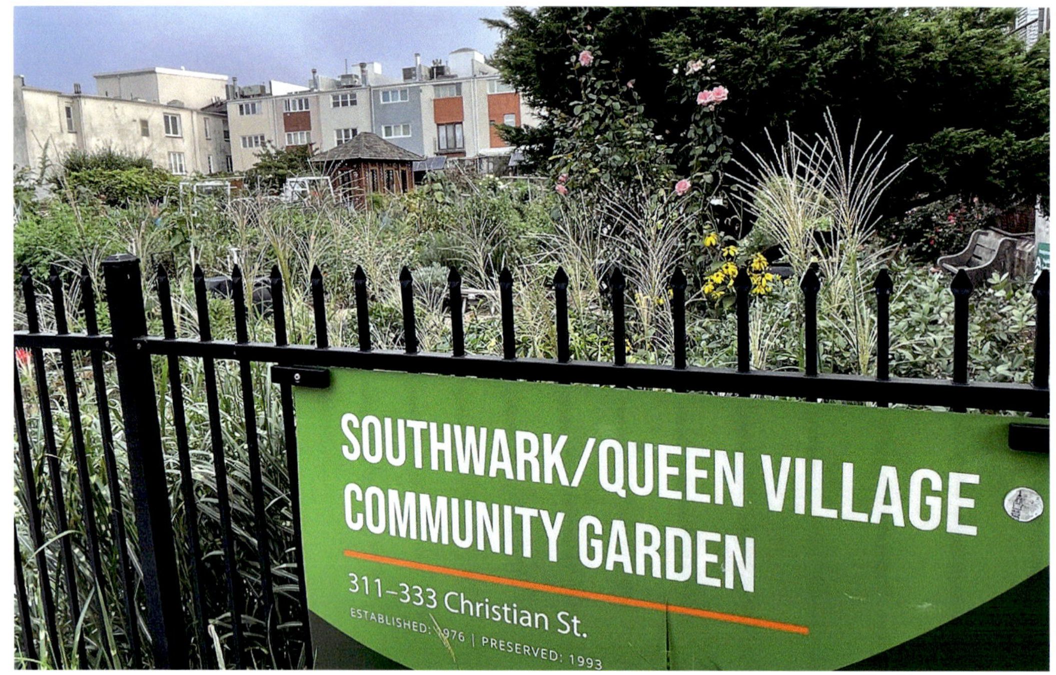

The Southwark/Queen Village Community Garden at Fourth and Christian Streets was the Ebenezer Church Burial Ground (est. 1810). The church closed in 1902 and the majority of the bodies were moved to Arlington Cemetery in Drexel Hill, Delaware County, PA.

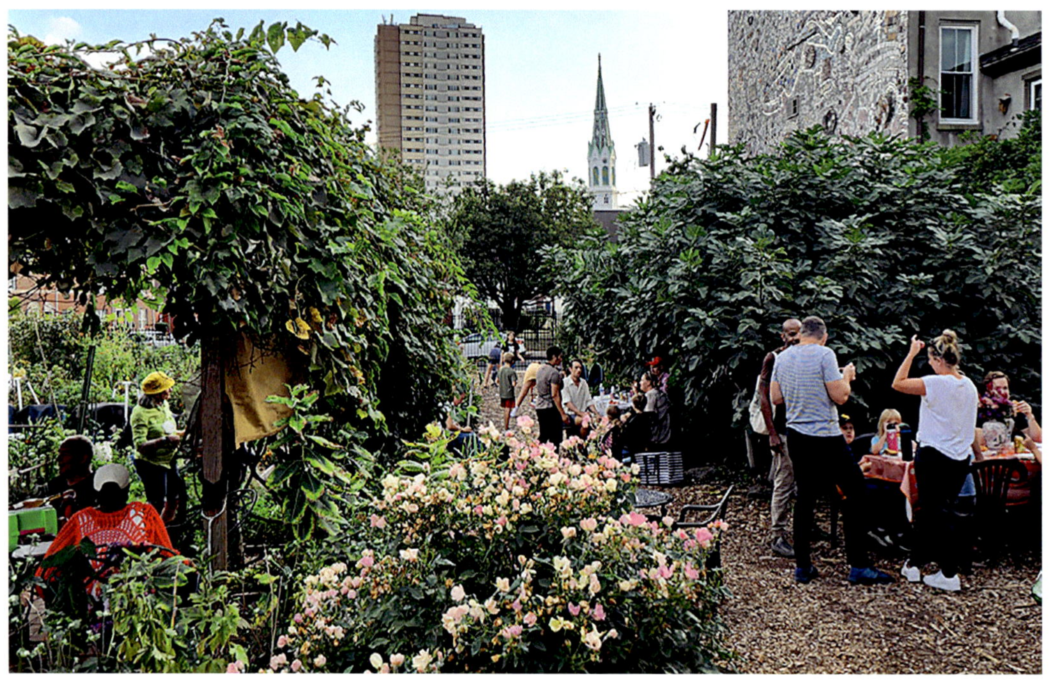

Neighborhood gardeners enjoying the fall festival in the Southwark/Queen Village Community Garden at Fourth and Christian Streets in September 2024. The property is repurposed land that had been the Ebenezer Church Burial Ground. (*Photo by Paul Wismar*)

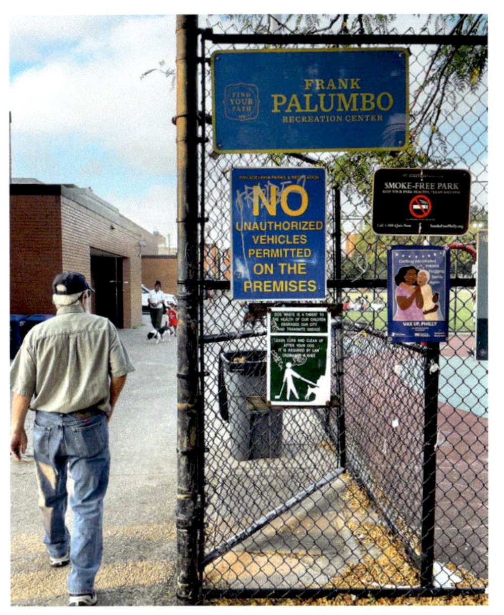

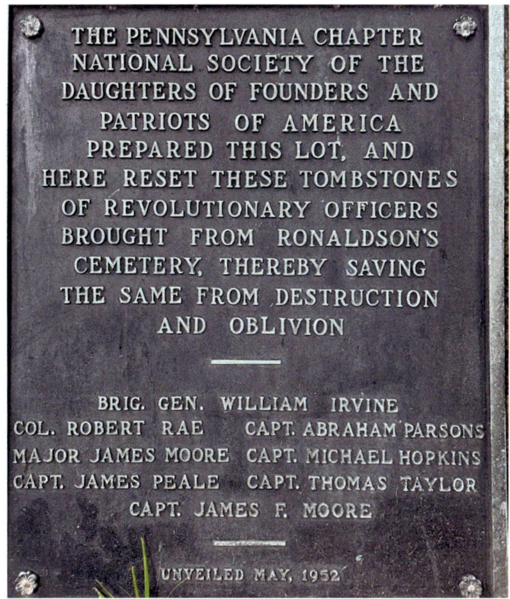
THE PENNSYLVANIA CHAPTER
NATIONAL SOCIETY OF THE
DAUGHTERS OF FOUNDERS AND
PATRIOTS OF AMERICA
PREPARED THIS LOT, AND
HERE RESET THESE TOMBSTONES
OF REVOLUTIONARY OFFICERS
BROUGHT FROM RONALDSON'S
CEMETERY, THEREBY SAVING
THE SAME FROM DESTRUCTION
AND OBLIVION

BRIG. GEN. WILLIAM IRVINE
COL. ROBERT RAE CAPT. ABRAHAM PARSONS
MAJOR JAMES MOORE CAPT. MICHAEL HOPKINS
CAPT. JAMES PEALE CAPT. THOMAS TAYLOR
CAPT. JAMES F. MOORE

UNVEILED MAY, 1952

Above left: Palumbo Recreation Center at Ninth and Fitzwater Streets had been Ronaldson's Cemetery from 1826–1950; it was then turned into a park. Its 14,000 inhabitants were moved to a suburban cemetery in northeast Philadelphia. Ronaldson's, possibly the nation's first private non-sectarian cemetery, was founded by James Ronaldson, one of the founders of the Franklin Institute.

Above right: At the closing of Ronaldson's Cemetery, several interred Revolutionary War Soldiers' graves and markers were relocated to the Old Swedes Church graveyard in Queen Village. Among those buried in Ronaldson's were John Stowers, said to have crossed the Delaware with George Washington and Commodore Charles Stewart, commander of Old Ironsides during the War of 1812.

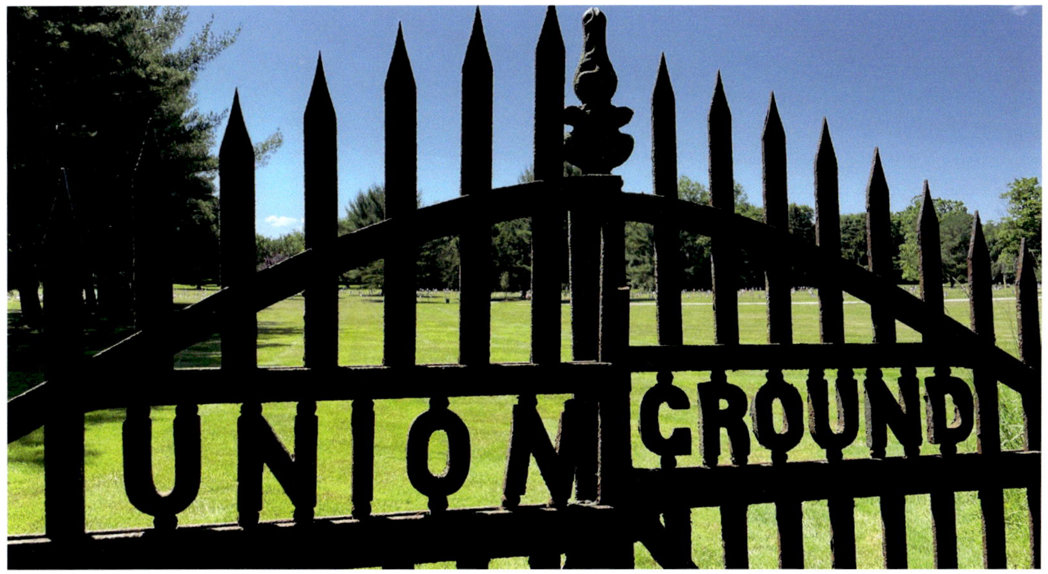

The original entrance gate from the 1842 Union Burial Ground at Sixth Street and Washington Avenue stands in an unmarked field at Philadelphia Memorial Park, Frazer, PA. It was moved in 1970 along with the graves of friendless seamen who died at the port of Philadelphia.

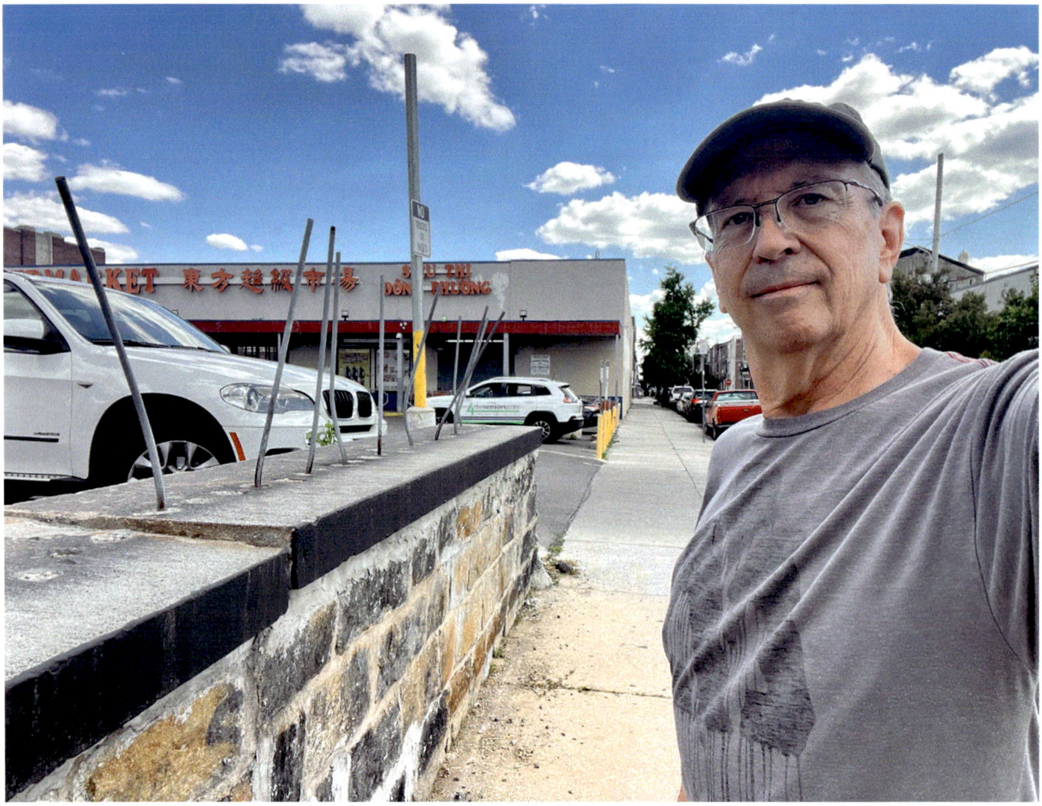

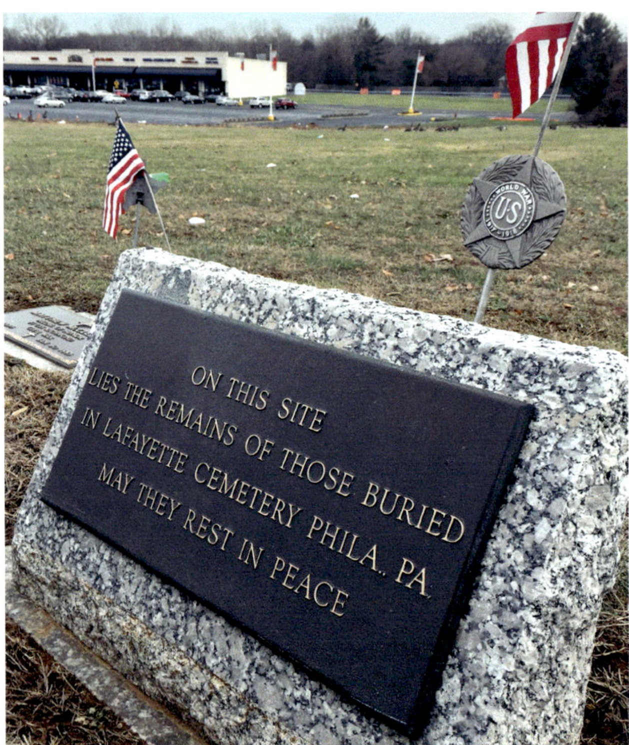

Above: The graves of about 2,000 people were moved from the Union Burial Ground in 1970 to make room for a supermarket, strip mall, and parking lots. The cemetery's original retaining wall remains intact.

Left: In a grassy field opposite a strip mall in the Philadelphia suburb of Bensalem, sits a small memorial flanked by two military grave markers, honoring the 47,000 graves that were accidentally found here in 1988. The remains were unceremoniously relocated here from the closed Lafayette Cemetery in 1946. Currently, the cemetery site is the location of the Capitolo Playground at Ninth and Federal Streets.

2

CITY V. RURAL CEMETERIES AND THE DEMISE OF LAFAYETTE CEMETERY

Philadelphia achieved its highest population density around 1950, and its people wanted parks, recreation, and other amenities, so old dilapidated cemeteries became land grab targets. After the establishment of large suburban cemeteries (e.g. Philadelphia Memorial Park in Frazer, PA, and Lawnview Cemetery in northeast Philadelphia), many smaller inner-city burial grounds were relocated to these locations. According to Doug Mooney, president of the Philadelphia Archaeological Forum, the relocations of these graves were usually not handled as one might expect.[1] Mooney states that he had been involved in more than a dozen cemetery excavations and had not found a single one in which all the graves were moved. He made the sobering observation that while a written record may exist, indicating that bodies were moved, this does not mean they were.

In nearby New Castle, Delaware, when the state buried 85 percent of Farnhurst Potter's Field to build Interstate 295 in 1958, the grave markers were left upright and buried under 15 feet of dirt. Perhaps burying them deeper, as opposed to disturbing the remains, was more ethical than what Philadelphia did to Lafayette Cemetery in 1946. In this case, the city did not even care where the contractor moved the bodies. Lafayette became the Capitolo Playground near the city's famous cheese steak emporiums.

Lafayette Cemetery, with its 47,000 burials, had been established in 1839 and saw its last burial in 1942. It was not being maintained. In 1946, the city condemned the cemetery as part of a multimillion-dollar playground-building project. The individual with whom the city contracted to remove the bodies and rebury them in the suburbs, didn't do what he was supposed to do. Thomas A. Morris, president of

Evergreen Memorial Park in Bensalem Township outside Philadelphia, was to move the bodies and grave markers, in exchange for clear title to the 4.2 acres of land. He moved what appears to be a majority of the bodies, sold the land to investors who then sold it back to the city! Until 1988, no one really knew what he did with the bodies, or apparently cared.

Morris dumped most of them into unmarked trenches on the outskirts of his Evergreen property in Bensalem. The only reason the public is aware of this is because of an accidental unearthing of some wooden coffins on the old Evergreen site in 1988. A strip mall was being built, and thousands of graves were discovered during its construction.[2] At some point after the investigation was completed, a monument of sorts was installed in the middle of the grassy field.

Satisfied with Morris' work, the city contracted with him again in 1947 to remove 8,000 bodies from Franklin Cemetery in Kensington. The remains were to be reburied in a 3-acre Franklin section of Evergreen. No tombstones were erected on the graves. Evergreen went bankrupt in 1961 and eventually became the current day Rosedale Memorial Park.

It may seem that the eradication or moving of city cemeteries to rural areas would have been a series of well planned and executed projects, but the situation described above is more the norm. It is also worth noting that neighbors witnessed the excavations. They had to tolerate the sights, sounds, and smells associated with the removal of remains. Eyewitnesses recall putrid summertime odors and in the case of Lafayette Cemetery, emotional crowds following truckloads of unearthed coffins as they were driven up the road, away from the cemetery.

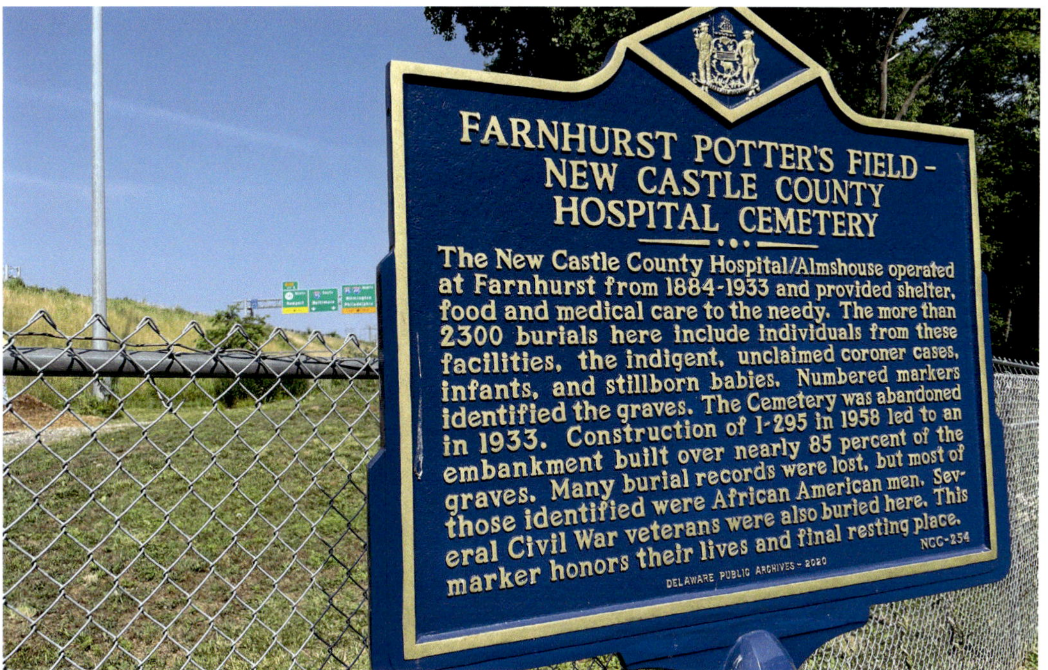

New Castle, Delaware's Farnhurst Potters' Field was in operation from 1884 until it was abandoned in 1933. The city buried most of the 2,300 graves in 1958 when it built the Interstate 295 highway over it.

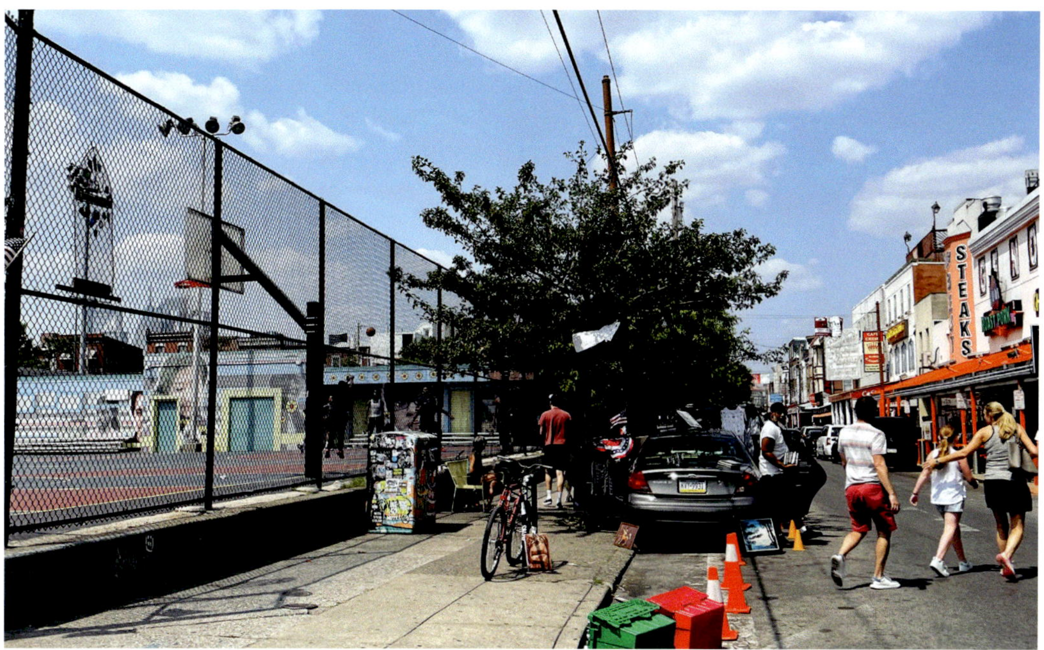

Sports and cheese steaks, two of Philadelphia's favorite things bring locals and tourists to Capitolo playground at Ninth and Federal Streets. In the 1940s, kids would buy potatoes from the local huckster and take them into Lafayette Cemetery, build a small fire, and bake the potatoes to eat. Others would play baseball in the old, run-down graveyard, probably using broken headstones as bases. The city removed the graves and stones from the property in 1946.

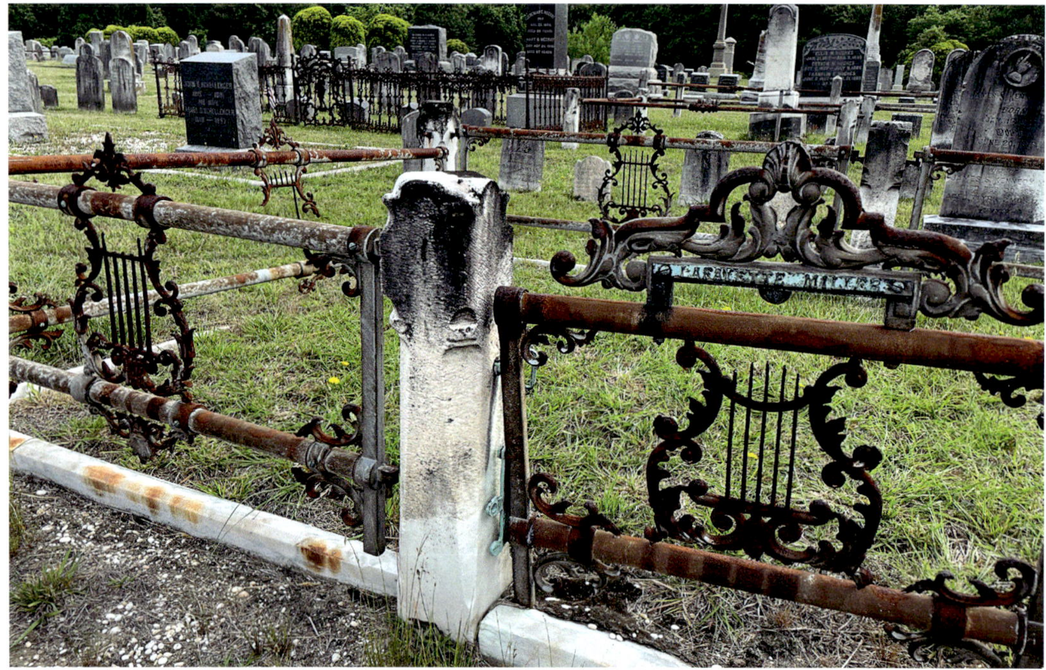

Victorian cemetery fencing was quite popular until the 1940s and served the purpose of delineating the particular plot. The cheap white metal was seen as an embarrassment to descendants and therefore much of it in the Philadelphia area was removed and discarded.

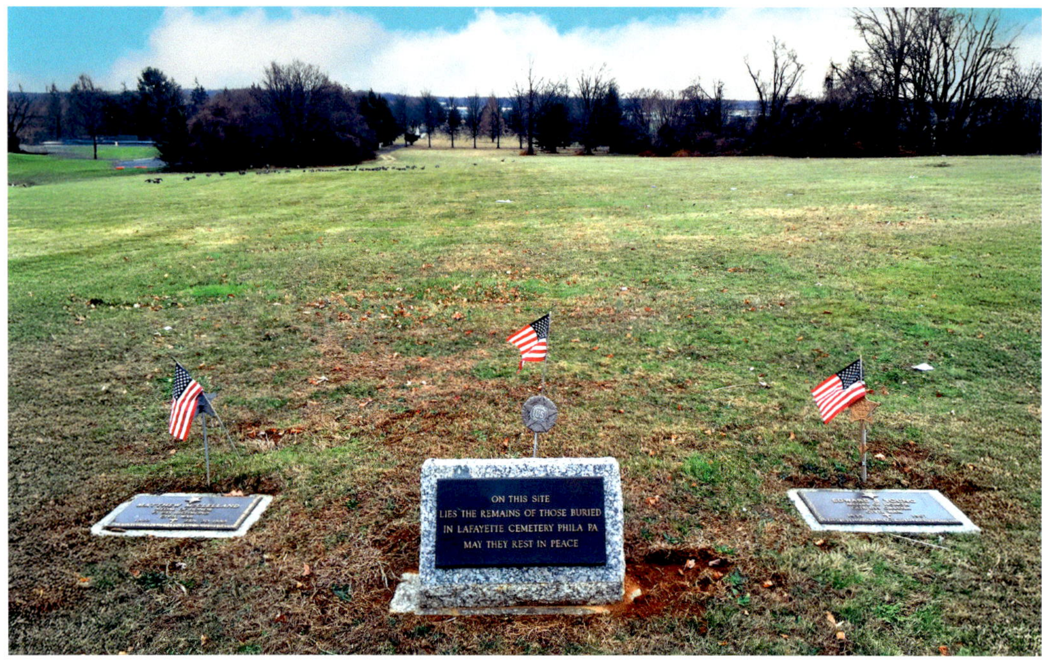

The man contracted by the city to move the graves from Lafayette Cemetery, Thomas Morris, was to rebury the bodies on 40 of the 156 acres owned by Evergreen Memorial Park, complete with caskets, drainage, new bronze markers, roadways and perpetual maintenance of the grounds. Instead, Morris dug trenches on the outskirts of his property and deposited the bodies in a giant unmarked mass grave.

3

THE WATERY REMAINS OF MONUMENT CEMETERY

Along the Delaware River waterfront under the Betsy Ross Bridge lie the remains of a cemetery. Scores of granite headstones, monuments, and ironwork lie on the shore, protrude from the embankment, and peek out of the murky river water. At low tide, the majority of grave markers can be seen.

Monument cemetery was located at Broad and Berks streets, near Temple University. It was the city's second Victorian rural garden cemetery, established in 1838, just after Laurel Hill (1836). With its Gothic-style gatehouse and central monument to Generals Washington and Lafayette, the cemetery grew to a fairly large size (28,000 graves over 15 acres).[1] The last burial plot was sold in 1929, and by 1938, the cemetery was full and had fallen into disrepair. No burials, no income. By the 1950s, Temple University, across the street, wanted it for a parking lot. Temple held public hearings and worked with the city to condemn the property so the school could purchase it. The picture painted was that Monument Cemetery was an eyesore, dangerous, and a blight on the neighborhood.[2]

At this point in history, the public was not keen on Victoriana (anything from the era 1837–1901). Many Victorian-era cemeteries fell into disrepair because people thought they were old fashioned. Lot owners removed the decorative plot fencing and other ironwork to dispose of or sell for scrap.

In 1956, remains were removed from the site (20,000 of which were reburied at Lawnview Cemetery in Rockledge, a northeastern suburb of Philadelphia) and most of the grave markers were dumped into the Delaware River. While most of the tombstones were used to buttress the shoreline at the foundation for what was to become the Betsy Ross Bridge, those of Temple founder Russell Conwell and his wife were moved (along with their remains) across the street to the Temple Campus.

Dozens of grave markers are strewn about the shore. Elegant granite stones glisten with moisture from just being under water. Border walls from family plots and huge blocks of foundation granite used for large monuments seem to have been the last objects that tumbled off the dump trucks, rolling over stones that had already been dumped. After 100 years, inscriptions are still clearly visible. These "grave markers" no longer physically mark the spot where the body is buried, but they still signify a life. They continue to have "agency," as Annette Stott says.[3] She suggests that such a stone has a direct bond to the dead person, a reassuring physicality that the person existed.

When notice was given to plot holders of the planned removal of the cemetery, as many as 8,000 bodies were relocated to various other cemeteries at their families' expense. The remaining 20,000 were moved to Lawnview Cemetery. Supposedly, the reburial records exist and are accurate. As one drives along the Lawnview property at the site of the mass grave, distinct furrows can be seen where the many trenches were dug to accommodate the bodies.[4] In 2012, Philadelphia psychic Valerie Morrison led an effort to relocate the grave markers to Lawnview, but this has not occurred. To breathe life into the people memorialized by these cenotaph stones, she and her staff researched and published biographies of the people whose stones lie at the river's edge.[5]

At the Pennsylvania Historical Society there is a three–volume set of documentation related to Monument Cemetery. In this set of burial records are tombstone inscriptions, an alphabetical listing of those interred, and legal documentation of the property. Also, there are dozens of copied newspaper clippings related to the battle to close the cemetery. Reading through these clippings, one better understands how a cemetery can be made to disappear.

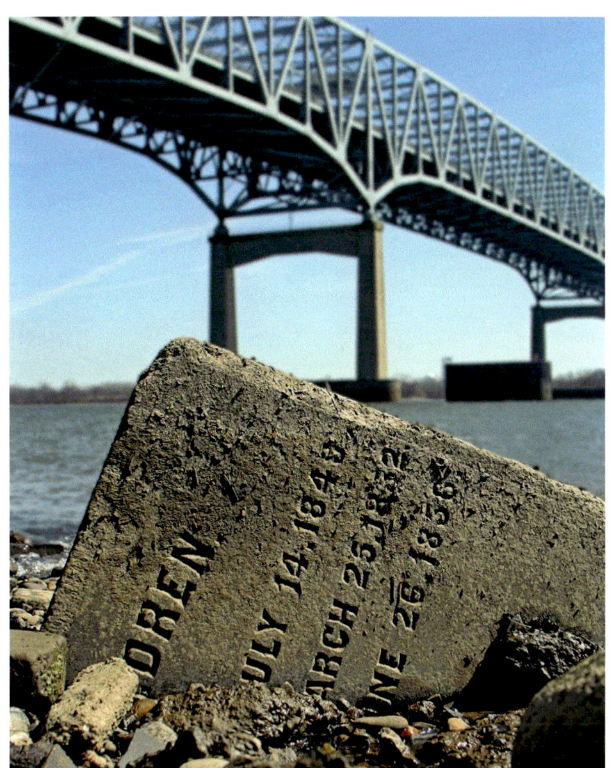

A child's grave marker is one of many stones visible on the shoreline of the Delaware River under the Betsy Ross Bridge. Many stones from Monument Cemetery were dumped here in 1956.

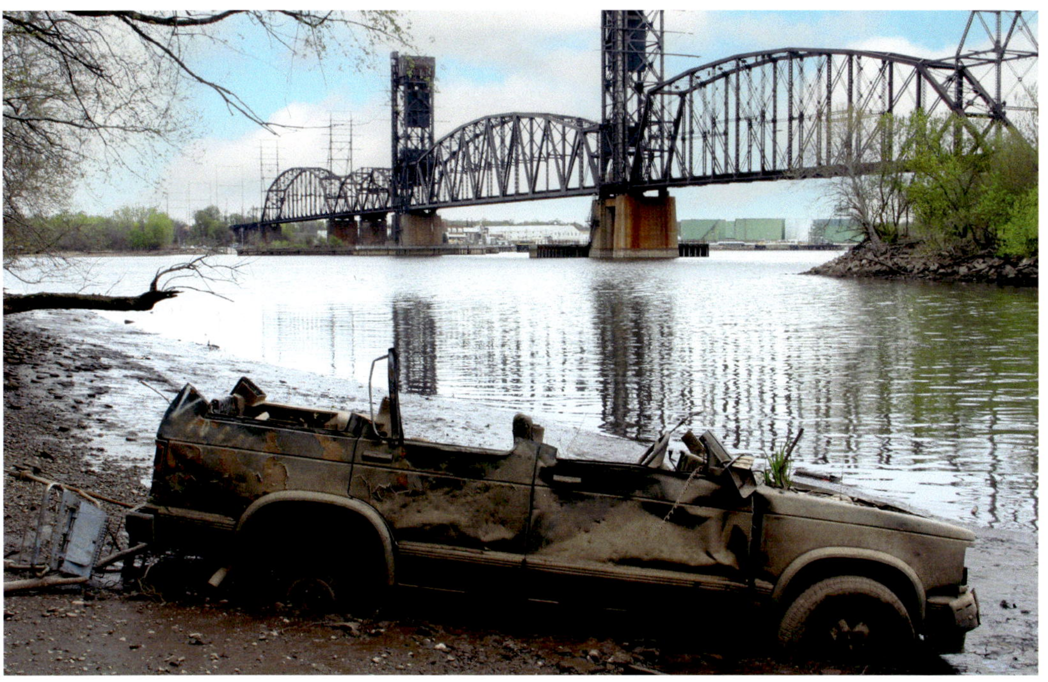

Frankford Creek empties into the Delaware River at Five Mile Point in the Bridesburg section of Philadelphia. At left is the land mass, or jetty, where the grave markers from Monument Cemetery lie.

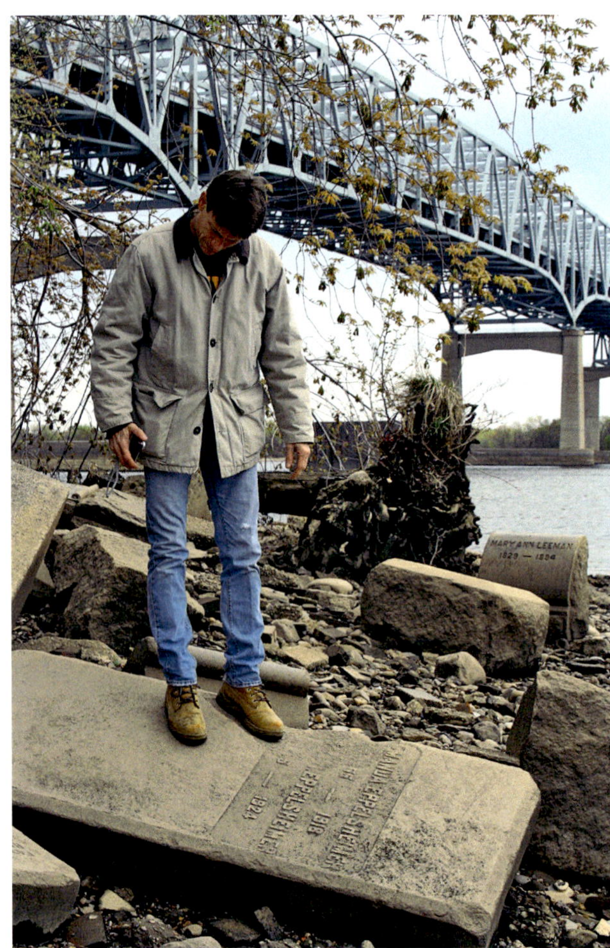

The grave markers on the river shoreline are all granite, which is a stronger stone than marble. Workers smashed the softer marble grave markers to pieces with sledgehammers in Monument Cemetery in 1956, reducing them to rubble, which was likely buried at the site.

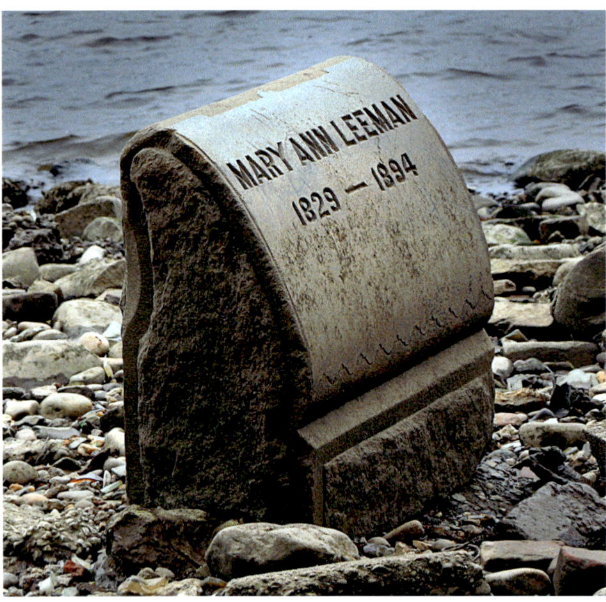

Mary Ann Leeman was married to Samuel Leeman, a sea captain. They had three children, Adelia, Lucy, and Frank. All had been born in Maine. One assumes they moved to Philadelphia because of this city's busy seaport. There are several Leeman stones at the riverfront, which may imply that the Leeman family plot was one of the last to be dismantled at Monument Cemetery. (www.valeriemorrison.com/newsletter.html)

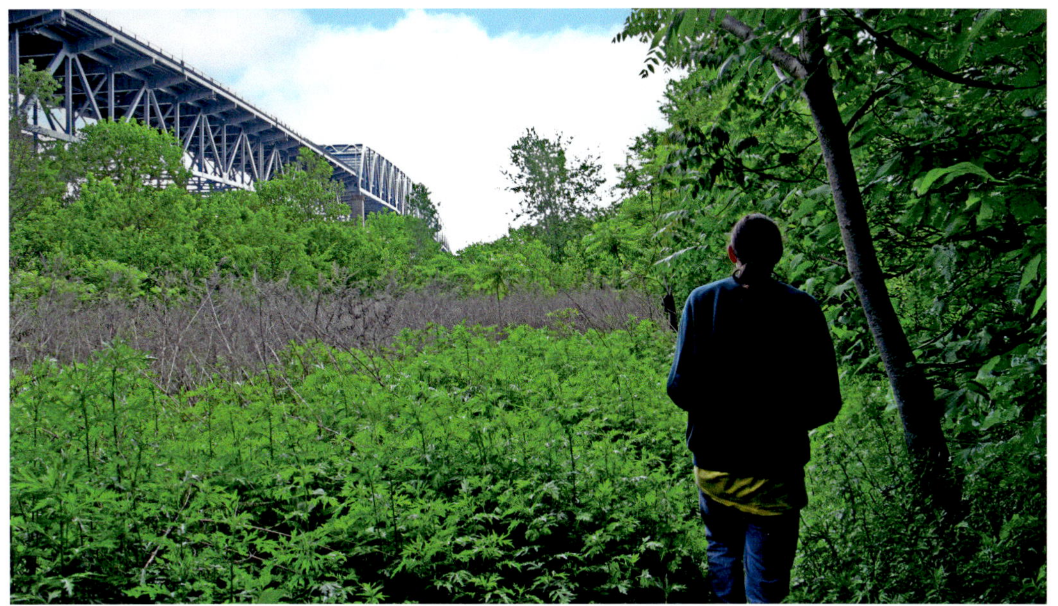

Access to the waterfront by land had been across a quarter-mile-long jetty under the Betsy Ross Bridge, between an abandoned power plant and an active industrial complex, until access was blocked with fencing. Prior to that, people walked through the weeds and woods to the water to fish here at Five Mile Point near the intersection of North Delaware Avenue and Lewis Street.

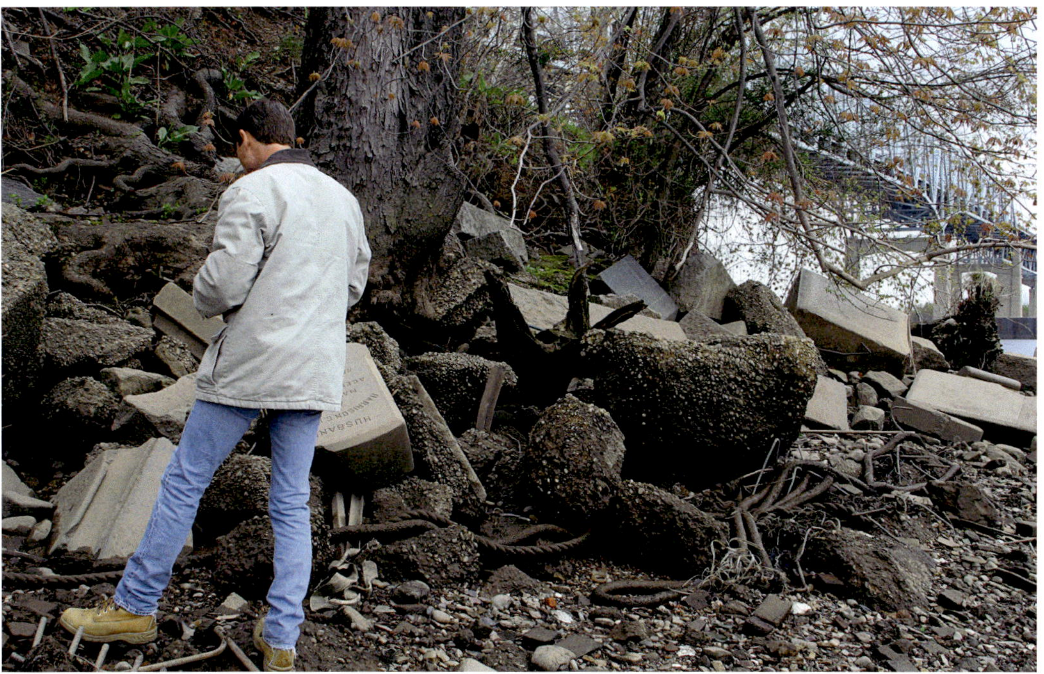

Pieces of monuments, whole headstones, plot border coping and other stonework from Monument Cemetery protrude from the embankment, the river floor, and the shoreline. Each name stares out like a cry for help. Even though many of Monument's lot owners fought the eviction of their ancestors, there really was not much public outcry against plowing over the cemetery and building a parking lot and athletic field, as Temple and the City's Board of Education wanted.

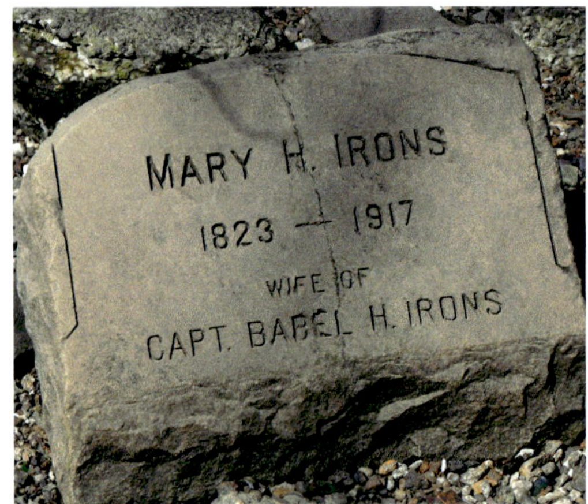

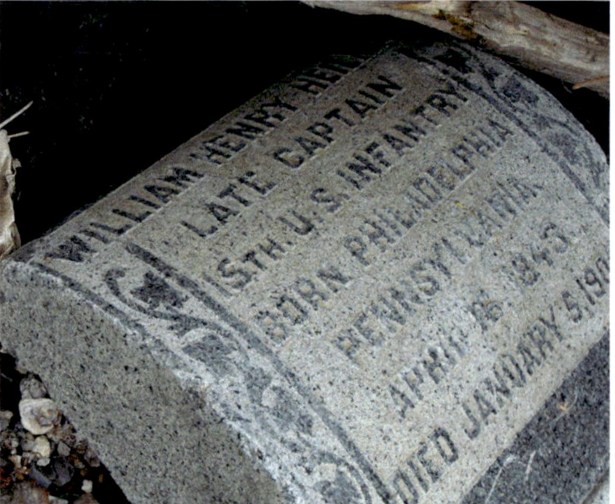

Above left: "Zorobabel Irons was a distant cousin of mine, and so I have come to this article in the process of doing family tree research. It grieves me to learn that Zorobabel's and Mary's remains and gravestones were treated with so little respect, but I thank you for honoring them in this blog post."—G. Netz, 2016. (*thecemeterytraveler.blogspot.com/2013/02/resting-in-pieces-along-delaware-river.html#comment-form*)

Above right: William Henry Heilman enlisted in the Union Army in 1861, at the age of eighteen. At the time he had gray eyes, brown hair, a light complexion and was 5 feet 8.5 inches tall. He fought in twenty-two major battles during the Civil War and reached the rank of captain when he resigned from duty in 1868. He was twenty-five years old. Granite does not fade like people's memories. (*www.valeriemorrison.com/newsletter.html*)

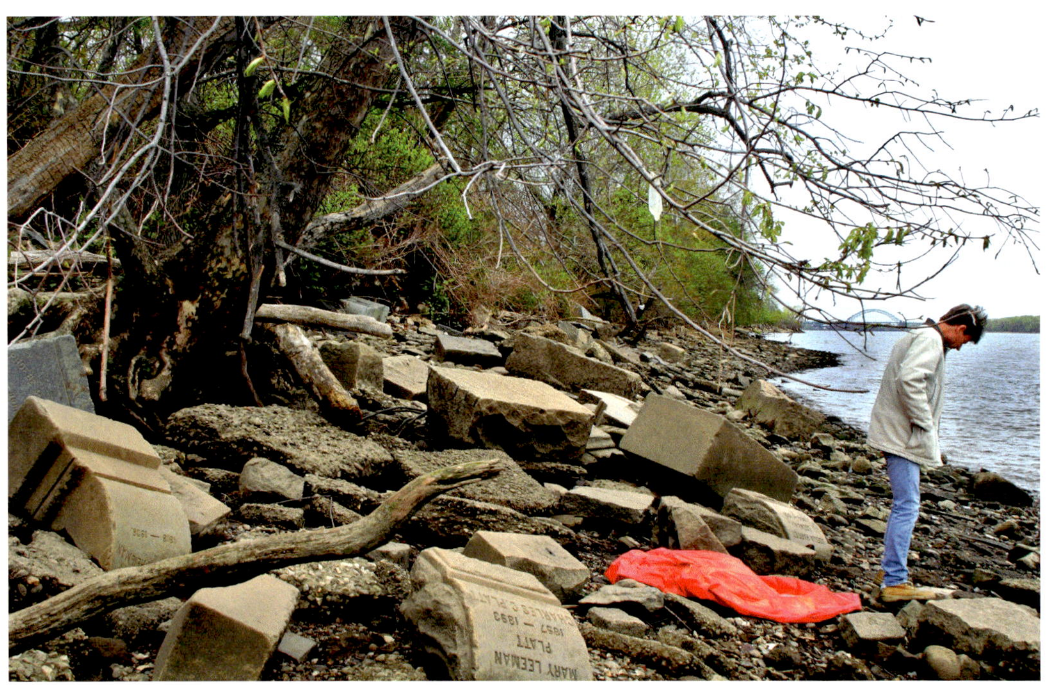

"Perhaps the world belongs to the living and the not-yet-living ... and Temple has been and remains the most-affordable, best-hope for higher education in Philadelphia. Isn't that worth more than a decaying cemetery?"—comment made on the author's "Cemetery Traveler" blog.

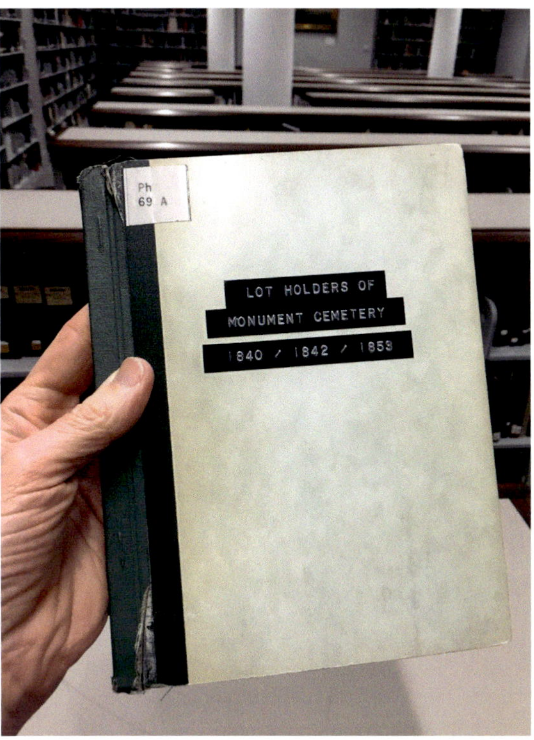

Burial records of Monument Cemetery are archived as bound volumes at the Pennsylvania Historical Society in Philadelphia. Included are newspaper clippings related to the removal of remains from the Cemetery. Twenty-five laborers manually removed 28,000 bodies over a five-month period during the summer of 1956. How scientific could that have been? The project supposedly resulted in exact identification of remains and their relocation to a distant suburban cemetery. Reburial records at Lawnview Cemetery are supposedly precise.

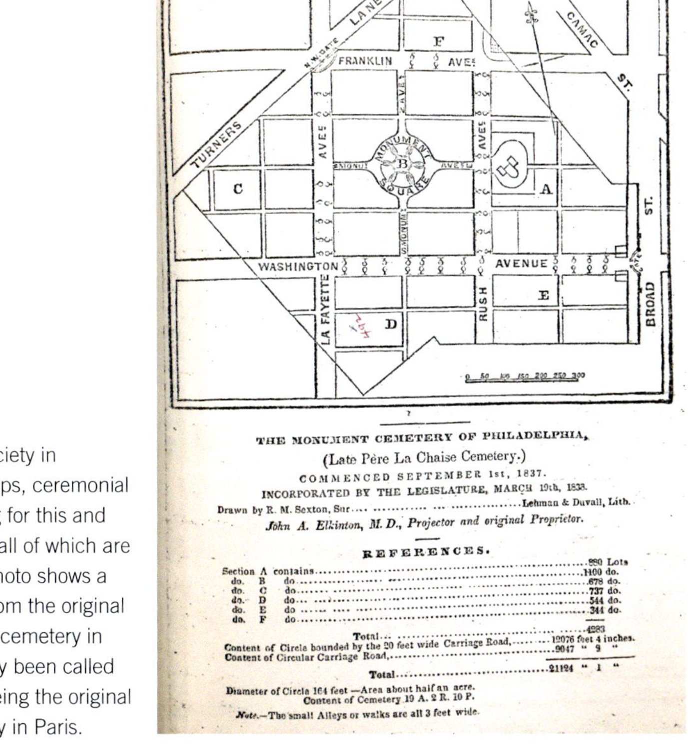

Ground Plot of Monument Cemetery.

THE MONUMENT CEMETERY OF PHILADELPHIA,

(Late Père La Chaise Cemetery.)

COMMENCED SEPTEMBER 1st, 1837.

INCORPORATED BY THE LEGISLATURE, MARCH 19th, 1838.

Drawn by R. M. Sexton, Sur........................Lehman & Duvall, Lith.

John A. Elkinton, M. D., Projector and original Proprietor.

REFERENCES.

Section A contains..........................880 Lots
do. B do..........................1100 do.
do. C do..........................678 do.
do. D do..........................737 do.
do. E do..........................544 do.
do. F do..........................344 do.

Total..........................4283

Content of Circle bounded by the 20 feet wide Carriage Road,..........12076 feet 4 inches.
Content of Circular Carriage Road,..........9047 " 9 "

Total..........................21124 " 1 "

Diameter of Circle 164 feet —Area about half an acre.
Content of Cemetery 19 A. 2 R. 10 P.

Note.—The small Alleys or walks are all 3 feet wide.

The Pennsylvania Historical Society in Philadelphia holds archived maps, ceremonial documentation, and advertising for this and other cemeteries of the region, all of which are available to researchers. The photo shows a map of Monument Cemetery from the original annual report published by the cemetery in 1838. The cemetery had initially been called Pere Lachaise, its namesake being the original 1804 Victorian garden cemetery in Paris.

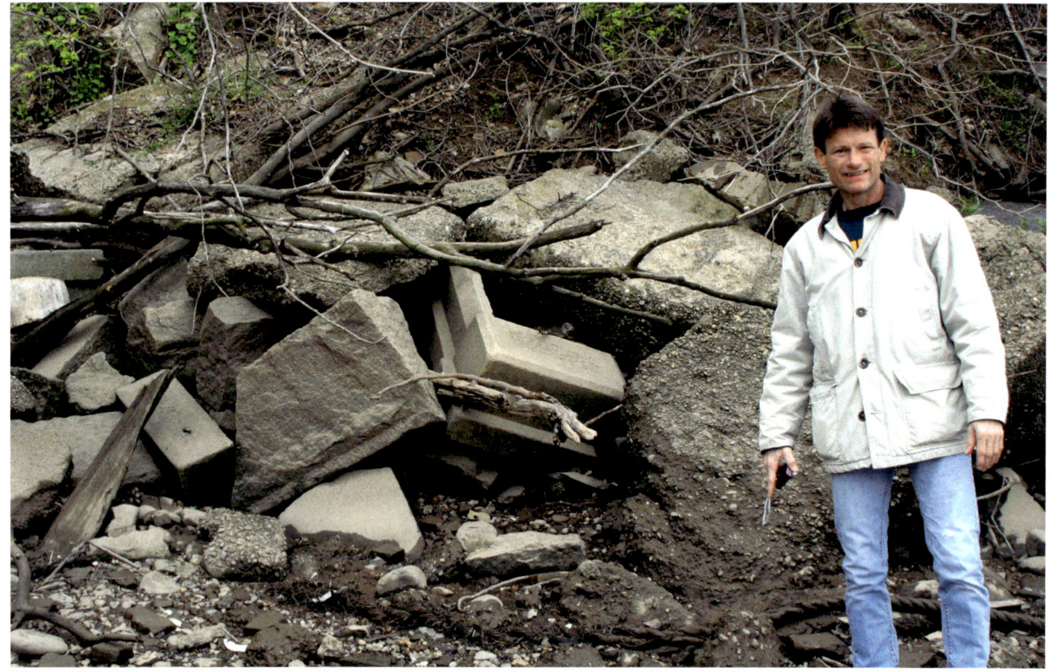

Most of the granite headstones, monuments, and other decorative stonework were dumped into the Delaware River as fill material to buttress the shoreline at the foundation for what was to become the Betsy Ross Bridge. While the 70-foot-tall central monument may be part of the jetty, there is other evidence that the cemetery existed, housed at the Library Company of Philadelphia and Pennsylvania Historical Society.

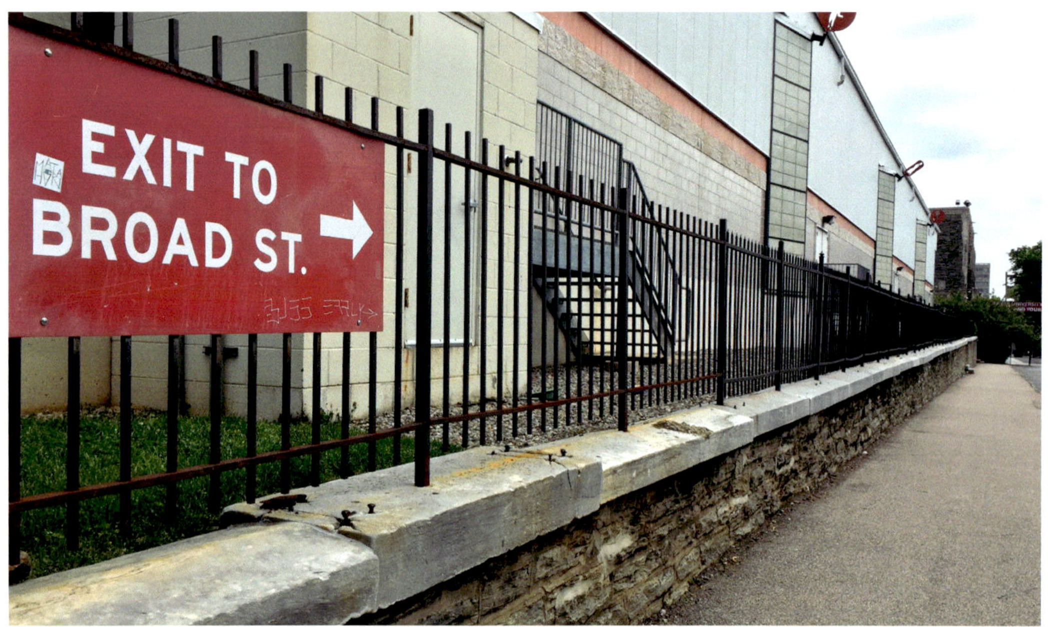

The original stone walls of Monument Cemetery remain, bordering Temple University's Geasey Field on Broad Street. There is no plaque or historical marker. There has been discussion since 2015 about Temple digging this up to build a new football field. If that ever happens, there is no doubt additional bodies will be found.

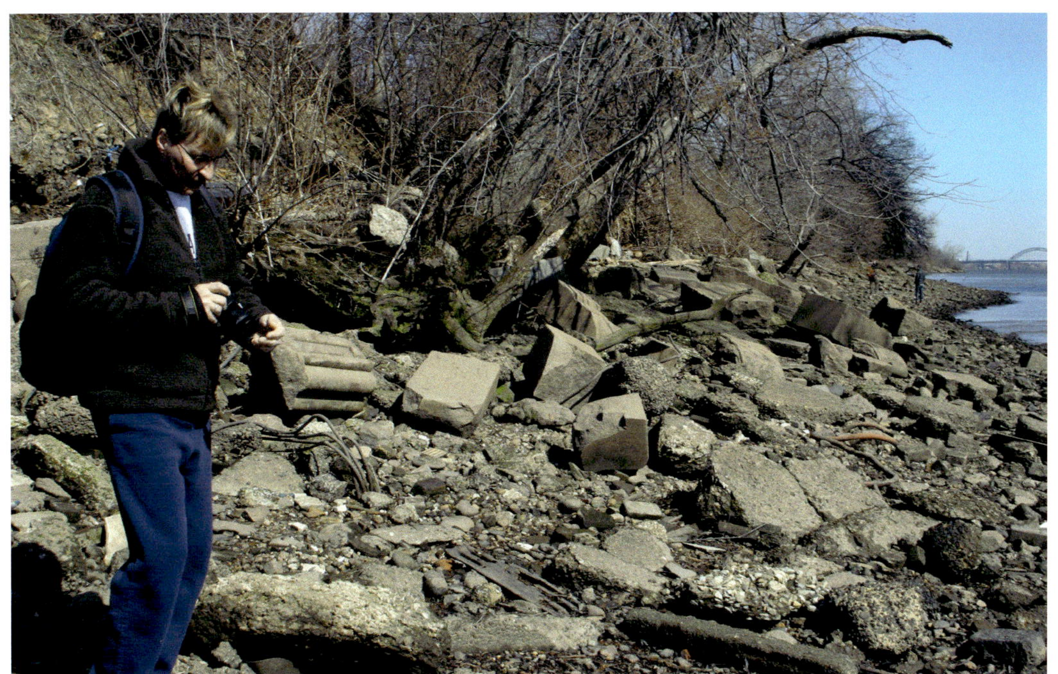

Above: Probing uncharted territory appeals to urban explorers—and those who vicariously enjoy the thrill through another's eyes. The interesting thing about abandoned locations is that they are often too dangerous for people to visit personally, so the general public's need is met through printed materials, videos, and social media.

Right: Walking along the riverfront among grave markers and monuments, shaded by trees hung with condoms and other trash, is like beachcombing in hell.

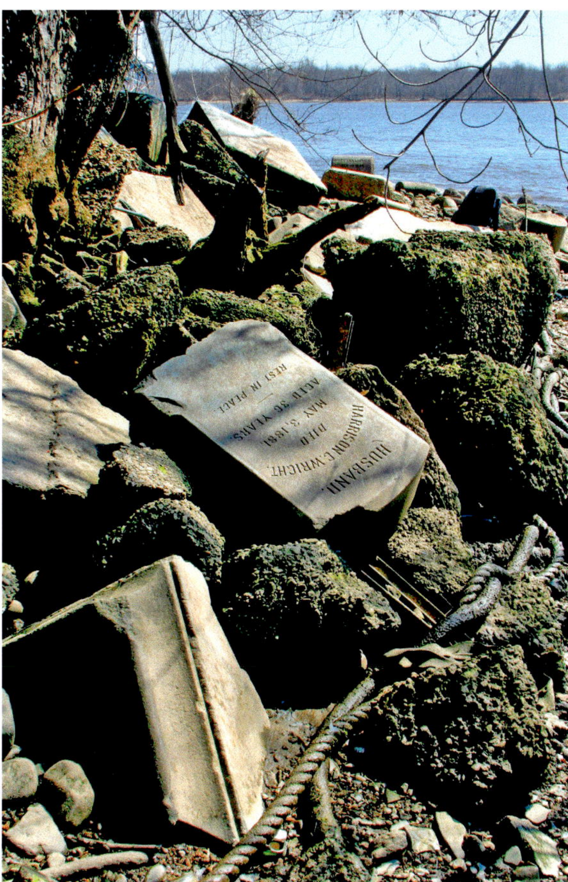

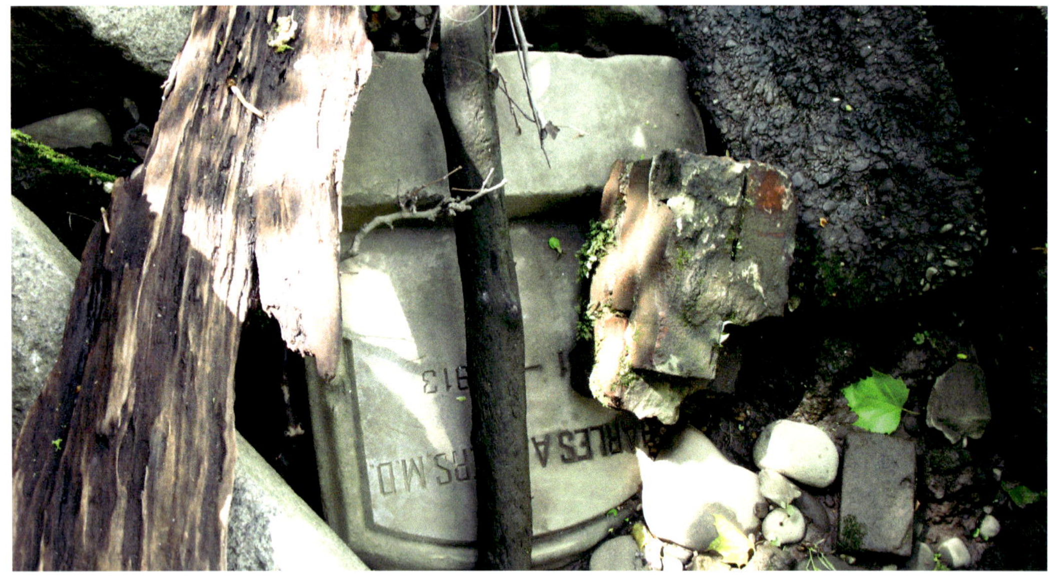

In 1954 when the cemetery owners sent out mailings to lot holders announcing that the graves would have to be moved when the cemetery was sold, they only had reliable contact information for 748 families—out of 28,000 burials. Only 400 lot holders responded to mailings, and 300 voted on which cemetery to move their ancestors to. People now consider adding stipulations to their burial contracts indicating that their remains never be disturbed.

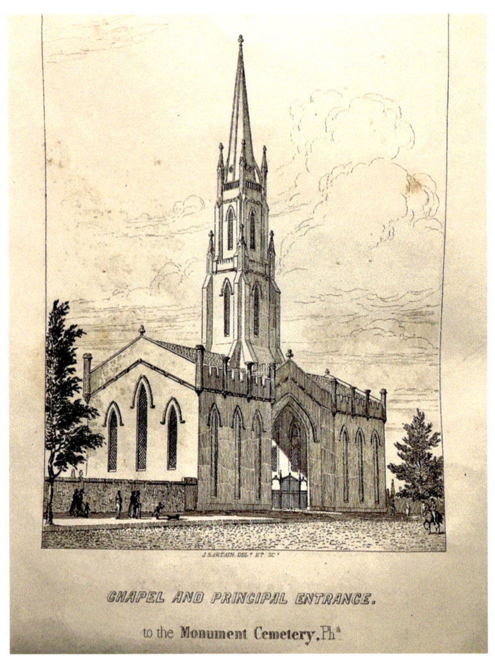

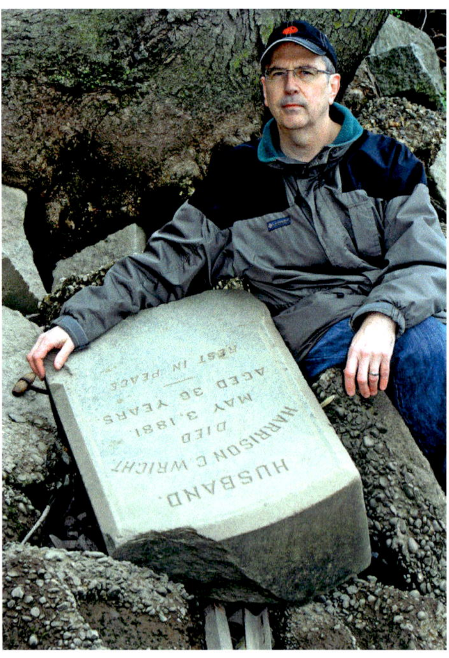

Above left: Both its gatehouse and central monument were designed by renaissance man John Sartain—artist, engraver, publisher, and friend of Edgar Allen Poe. The photo is from the 1852 Annual Report of the Monument Cemetery, Philadelphia. The gatehouse was demolished in 1902 so the city could extend Berks Street.

Above right: In our minds, a grave marker can take the place of the deceased person in the physical world. With the body gone, the stone is a physical manifestation of that person.

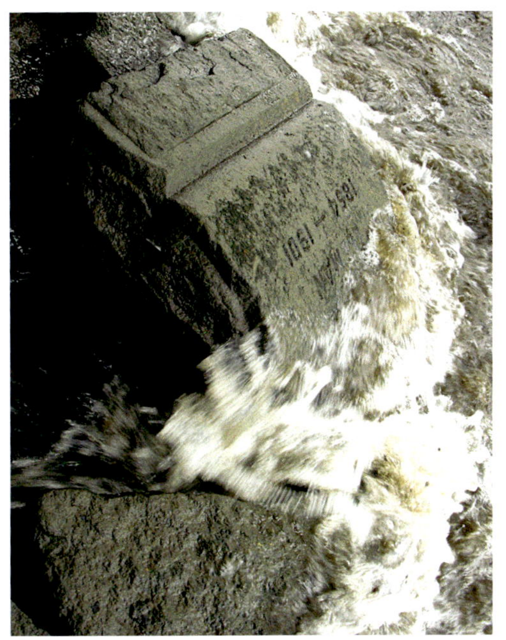

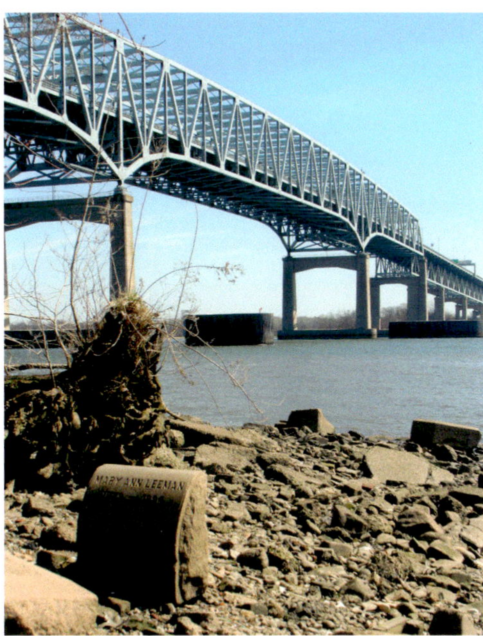

Above left: When the tide comes in on the Delaware River, many of the grave markers from Monument Cemetery are submerged under 6 feet of water.

Above right: The Betsy Ross Bridge extends from Philadelphia across the Delaware River to Pennsauken, New Jersey. It was opened in 1976. While the grave markers stretch along the shoreline for the length of a city block, they cannot be seen from the bridge.

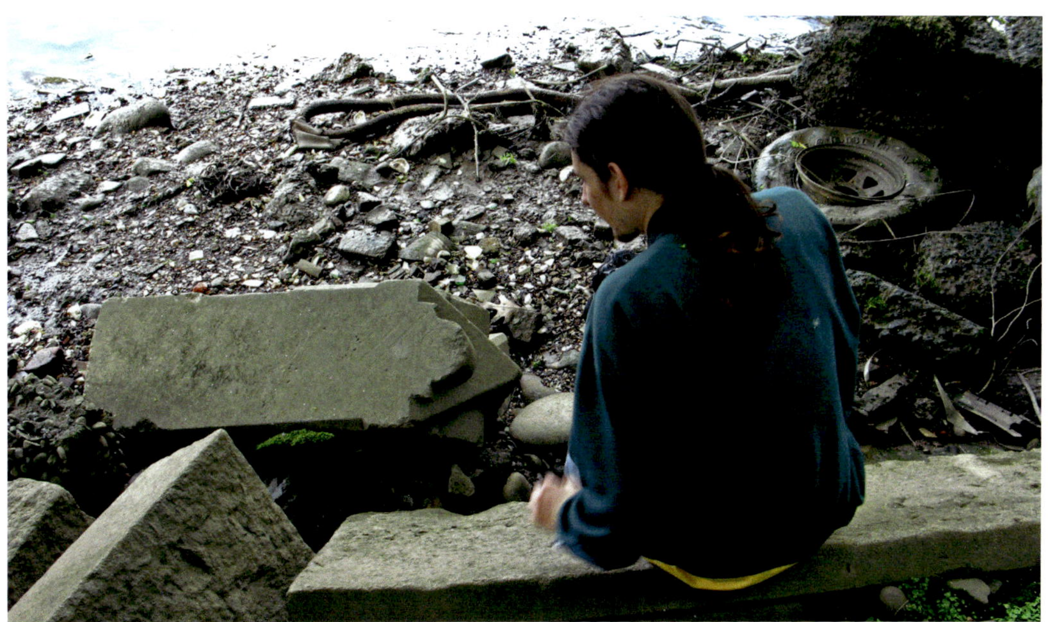

The City of Philadelphia likely acquired Monument Cemetery the same way it acquired other properties in 1956, through eminent domain. The properties it needed to build Independence National Historical Park in 1956 were acquired in this fashion.

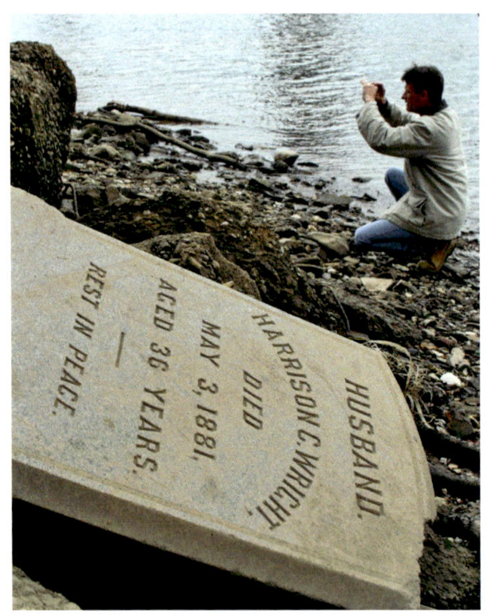

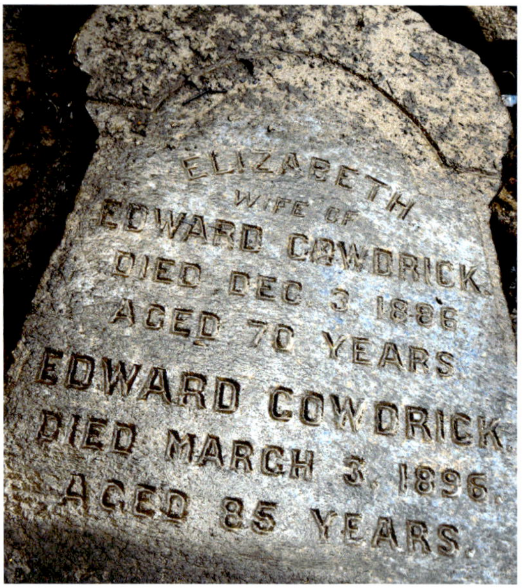

Above left: Instead of resting in peace, these gravestones are resting in pieces, as Philadelphia historian Tom Keels has said. While they no longer mark the graves at Monument Cemetery (or Lawnview Cemetery, where the bodies were supposedly reburied), they still exert a force on the viewer. The reburial records may be questionable, but the stones are not.

Above right: Victorians felt that the departed were expected to carry their headstones to heaven with them on Judgement Day to prove their identity, according to Bram Stoker in *Dracula*, Chapter VI, on Whitby Abbey Cemetery.

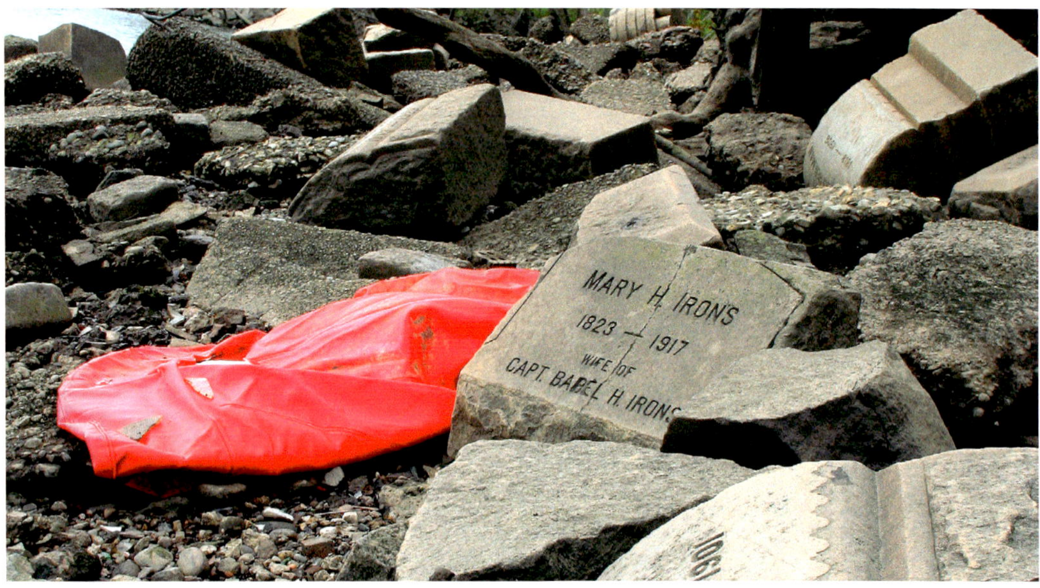

"I was a Temple student when bodies, aka remains, were removed from Monument.... Not all gravestones were removed. I remember marble ones being smashed to pieces by workers with sledge hammers. I also remember wooden coffins being opened by workers with hooks. The high water table had flooded these coffins and what remained of the bodies were extracted. I assume the wooden coffins, or what's left of them, remain underground to this day." (*thecemeterytraveler.blogspot.com/2011/05/how-monument-cemetery-was-destroyed.html*)

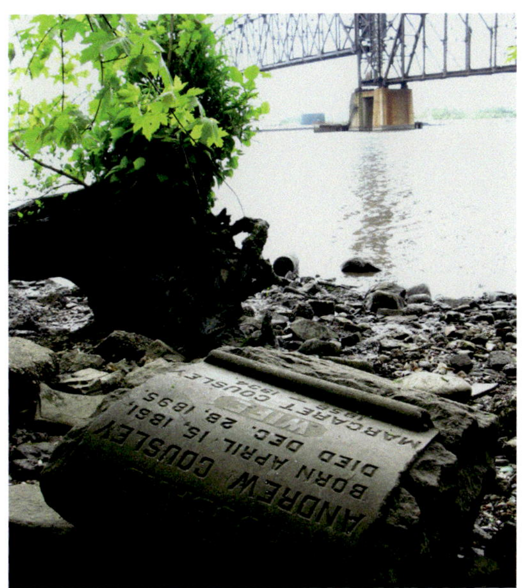

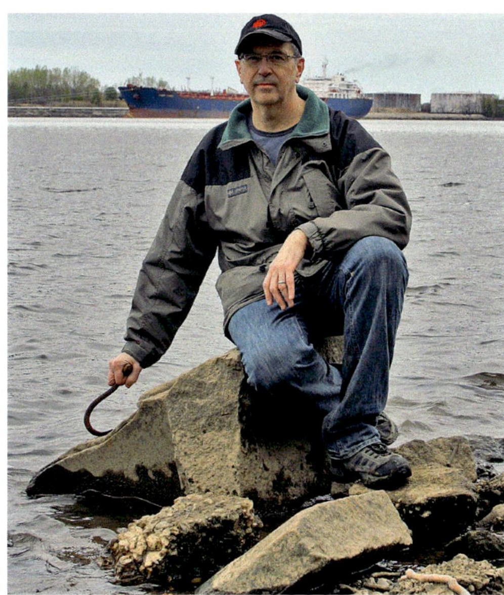

Above left: The names would be obscured until the next low tide, but because of current public interest in what happened to Monument Cemetery, their memory lives on in ways they never could have expected.

Above right: Why do canoeists floating over these grave markers in the Delaware have an uneasy feeling, as they look down at names and dates? The stones exert agency through an ability to stimulate both aesthetic and intellectual responses, according to Annette Stott, in her paper, "Personhood and Agency: A Theoretical Approach to Gravemarkers in Mainstream American Cemeteries," Markers, Vol. XXXV, Association for Gravestone Studies (Sterling Printing, 2019).

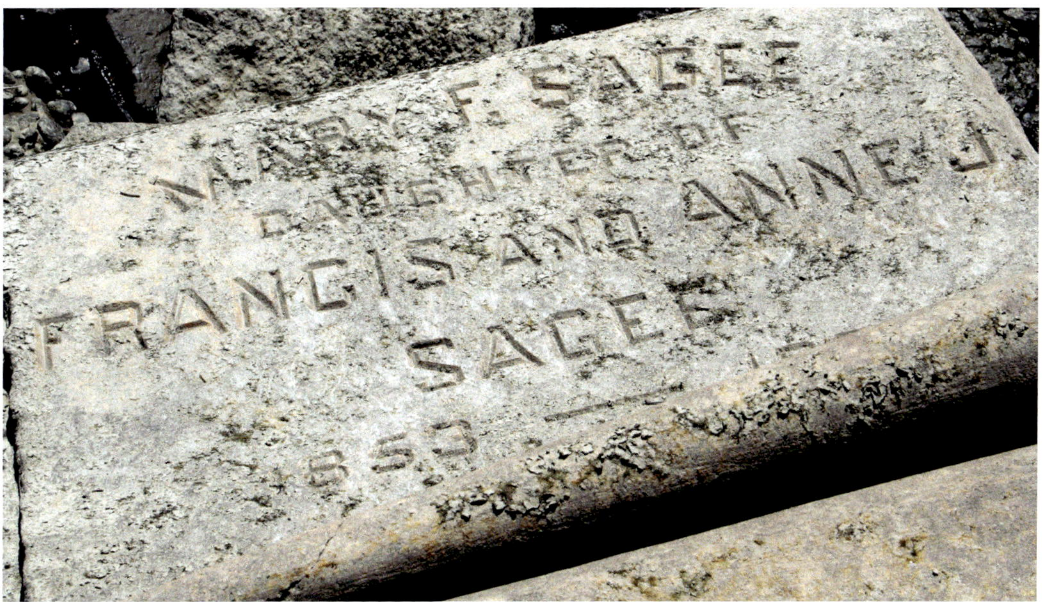

Mary Sagee was a schoolteacher, having attended the Girls Normal School beginning in 1870. "Normal" Schools referred to schools that educated future teachers to work in the Philadelphia public school system. The particular school Mary attended was later renamed Philadelphia High School for Girls, or as it is referred to today, Girls High. (*www.valeriemorrison.com/newsletter.html*)

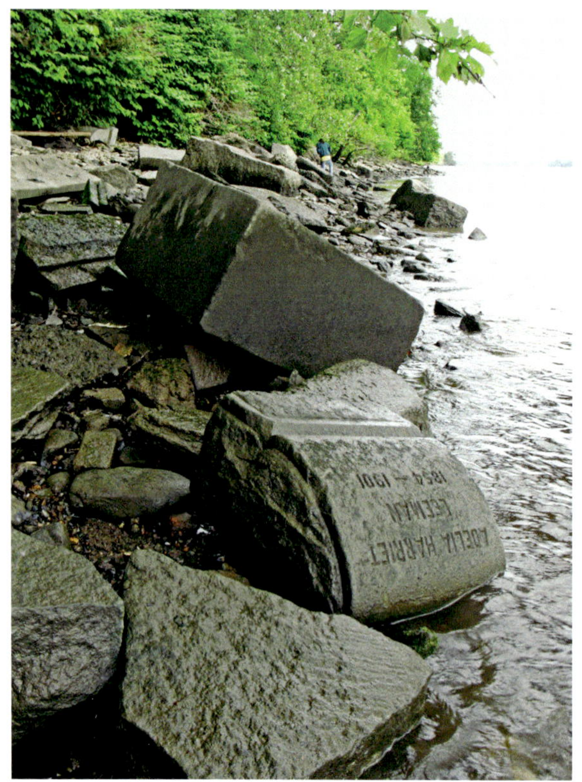

Normally, one need not check tide tables before visiting a cemetery. However, low tide is the best time to see grave markers from Philadelphia's defunct Monument Cemetery, as most of the stones are covered by 6 feet of water at high tide. (*saltwatertides.com/dynamic.dir/delawareriversites.html*)

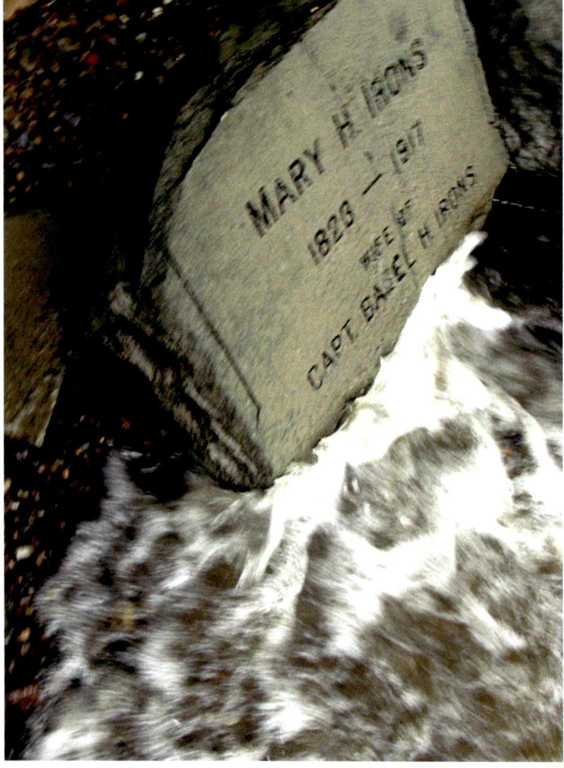

"... her highborn kinsmen came and bore her away from me, to shut her up in a sepulchre in this kingdom by the sea."—Annabel Lee, Edgar Allen Poe, 1849. Philadelphian John Sartain (1808–1897), buried in Monument Cemetery, published several of Edgar Allen Poe's works in his *Union Magazine* (1848–1852). "It appears that the last poem he ever wrote was the one entitled Annabel Lee. We purchased it from him..."—from *Reminiscences of a Very Old Man*, John Sartain, 1808–1897.

4

GENEALOGICAL CHALLENGES

Saving the Dead from Obstruction and Oblivion

Genealogical searches rely on birth, death, and burial records. The burial records associated with abandoned or non-existent cemeteries are notorious problems for genealogists. Prior to the era of digitizing records to online cloud-based databases, handwritten ledgers were the norm. Sometimes copies of these books were made and kept at local libraries and historical societies. Sometimes they were not. The Pennsylvania Historical Society in Philadelphia is home to a vast collection of burial records from many active and defunct cemeteries in Philadelphia and its environs.

Records can disappear. Mount Peace Cemetery, across the Delaware River from Philadelphia in Lawnside, New Jersey, lost all burial records and plot maps in 1952 in a cemetery office fire.[1] When Hurricane Agnes hit Pennsylvania's Wyoming Valley in 1972, the swollen Susquehanna River burst through the dike at Forty-Fort Cemetery (est. 1777) and washed away thousands of graves and monuments. Hours before the dike burst, the caretaker saved as many of the handwritten records as he could.

People may not realize that in terms of cemetery preservation, the care of burial records is part of the package. This became a massive surprise to the Friends of Mount Moriah Cemetery, Inc., when it gained access to approximately 150,000 records, some years after the property was abandoned in 2010. People have traveled thousands of miles to see the grave markers of their ancestors at Mount Moriah. If not for the burial records and the volunteers who research and photograph them for the requestors, these visits to the graves would not be possible.

Additional online tools for genealogical research are blogging and the www.findagrave.com website. Many cemetery-related blogs exist, including the author's own "Cemetery Traveler" blog.[2] Posting photos of gravestones can aid genealogical research because for many, a published photograph of a grave marker is a powerful historical link. Annette Stott describes such a stone as having a direct bond to the dead person, a reassuring physicality that the person existed.[3]

When a cemetery is sold or transferred to a new owner, one might assume that the records are now the responsibility of the new owner. If remains were moved to a different cemetery, that receiving cemetery should have the records. Also, descendants should have access to those records. What angers many people is when the receiving cemetery charges a fee to look up records and provide reburial information. This has happened often with Philadelphia cemeteries that have had bodies relocated from inner city cemeteries to those in the suburbs.

What happens to the records when cemeteries disappear? That all depends. When a religious congregation disbands, the burial records for its cemetery can be lost. If one large cemetery sells burial plots to many different churches, benevolent organizations, or professional societies, and those entities disappear, the records may be gone. American cities originally buried their dead in churchyards—if you were a congregant. You could be buried in a fraternal organization burial ground if you were a member. It was not until the 1820s that growing cities found the need for non-private, nonsectarian burial grounds.

If you died a pauper, a warehoused resident of a mental asylum, or simply died when you were passing through town, you were likely buried in a Potters' Field. Sometimes records are kept of Potters' Field burials, e.g. was done for the Delaware State Hospital, New Castle, Delaware. Philadelphia has no burial records for its most famous Potters' Field, Washington Square Park.

Potters' Fields are so named for the Bible story in which Judas, after betraying Jesus, hanged himself. The priests who had paid him to betray Jesus used the money to buy a plot of ground for his burial in a field where potters extracted red clay to make ceramic pottery. Judas would not have been allowed burial in any established ground. This potters' field was to be used for criminals, strangers, and the poor who could not be buried elsewhere.

Established as a Potters' Field by William Penn in 1706, it is unlikely that any of Washington Square Park's thousands of burials were recorded. Here in the historic district of the city, the park was originally used as a mass grave for thousands of British and American soldiers during the American Revolution. It saw continued use as a burial ground for strangers, criminals, yellow fever victims, and the poor up until 1815. Alexandra Mosca, in her article "Cemetery Bloggers," says that cemeteries are more than a final resting place, they hold secrets of the past.[4] Without burial records and other genealogical data, those secrets are forever hidden.

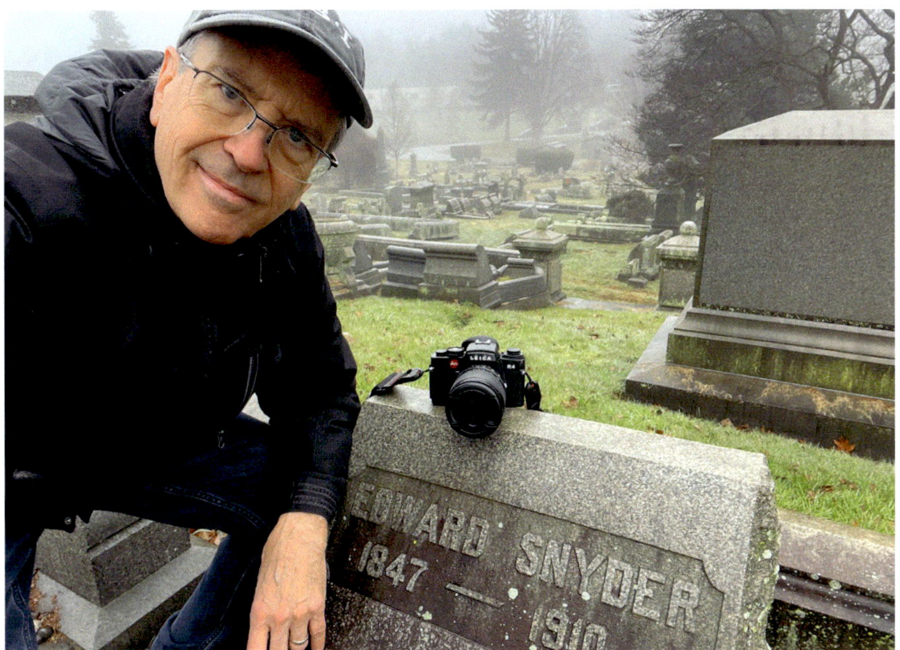

Genealogical research helps to preserve the past for future generations. While it has scholarly and forensic purposes, much of current marketing is focused on the individual. Perhaps we need a sense of our past, a more visceral sense of belonging, a more concrete sense of place in the larger human family. Genealogy has become massively popular in the twenty-first century.

Burial record books are archived at the Pennsylvania Historical Society at 1300 Locust Street in Philadelphia, which, oddly, was not built over an abandoned cemetery. A block away, however, at Thirteenth and Cypress Streets, the entire block had once been occupied by the Associate Presbyterian/St. Mary's Roman Catholic Burial Gound in addition to St. Luke's Protestant Episcopal Burial Ground. St. Luke's graves were never moved and have been paved over for local resident parking.

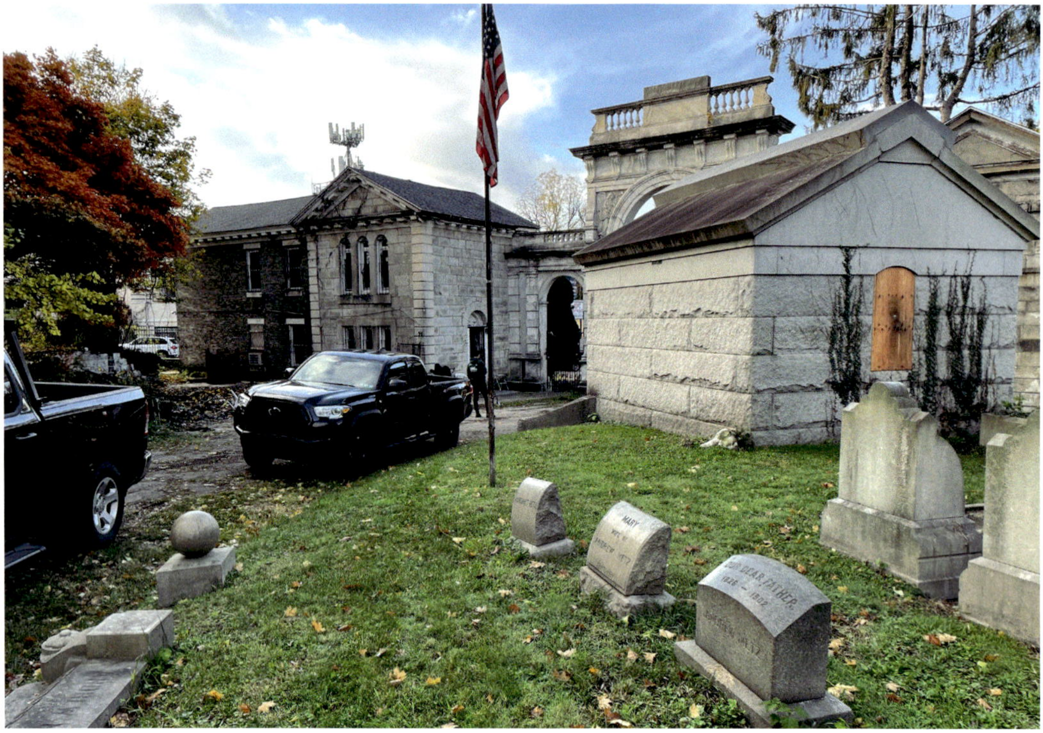

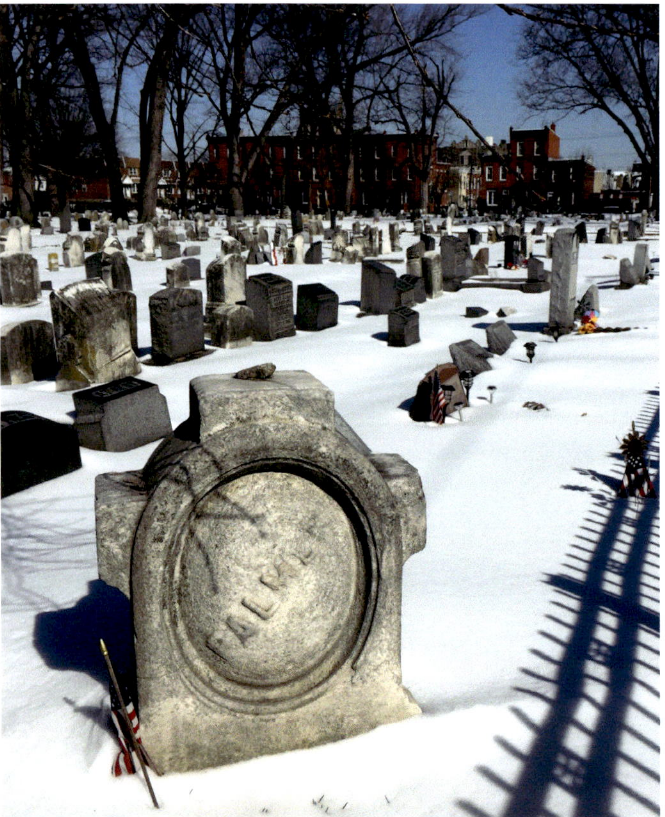

Above: The burial records stored at Mount Vernon Cemetery in Philadelphia were compromised when rain began leaking through the roof of the vacant office building around 2015.

Left: Even for cemeteries that still exist, such as the Palmer Burial Ground in Philadelphia's Fishtown neighborhood, records may not exist. For the first seventy years of its existence (established 1765), records were simply not kept. As singer Joni Mitchell says, we don't know what we've got 'til its gone.

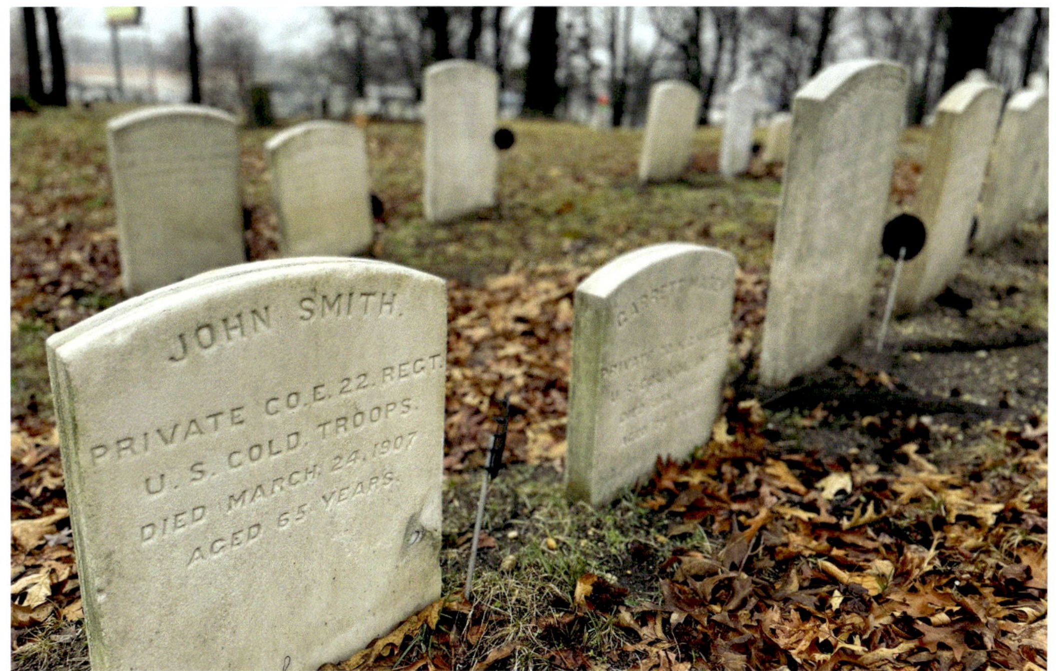

United States Colored Troops (USCT) stones mark the graves of 135 African American military veterans in Mount Peace Cemetery, Lawnside, New Jersey, who fought for the Union in the American Civil War. Their grave markers still stand, thanks to volunteer preservationists.

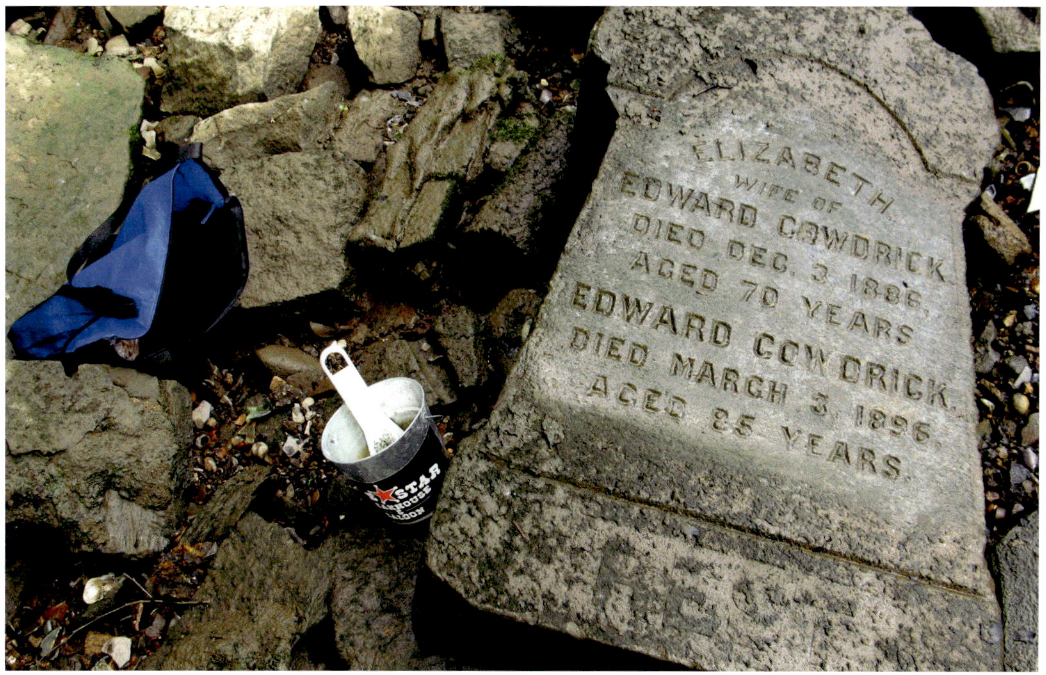

After several visits to photograph the grave markers under the Betsy Ross Bridge, many individuals requested that the author post these photographs and document the names, dates, and other inscriptions on www.findagrave.com, under the entry for Monument Cemetery. Some stones needed cleaning in order to accurately record the inscriptions.

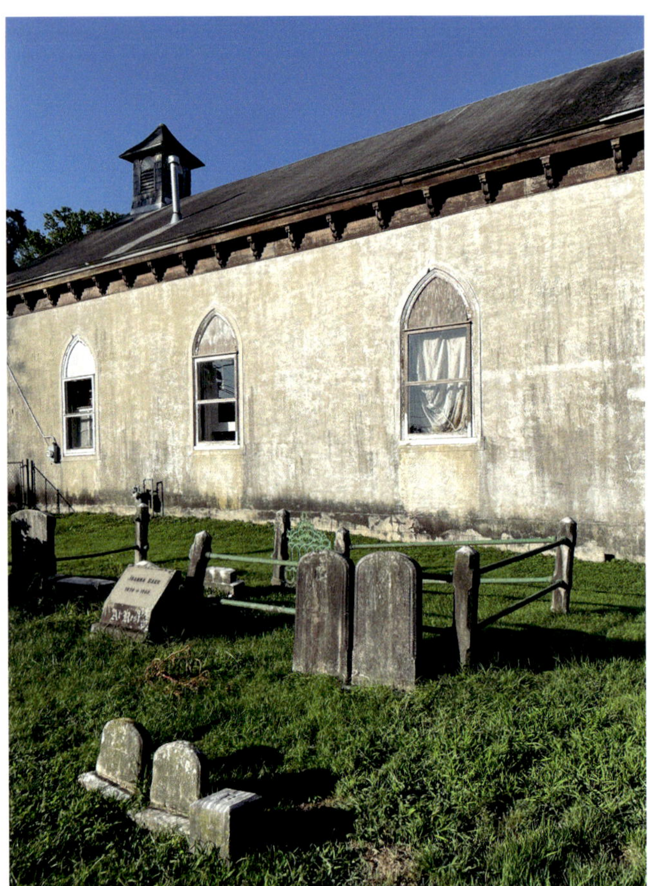

Left: Occasionally, a church is decommissioned, sold, then used for non-religious purposes e.g. a private home or commercial business. Perhaps the property comes with a graveyard, like the former Bethesda Methodist Church in Havertown, PA (Philadelphia suburb), which now houses art studios.

Below: The Delaware State Hospital Cemetery is on the hospital grounds in New Castle, Delaware. This was a formal mental hospital. Full body Potters' Field burials are the norm in Delaware while the indigent are cremated in Philadelphia. DNA and forensic testing are not possible with cremains.

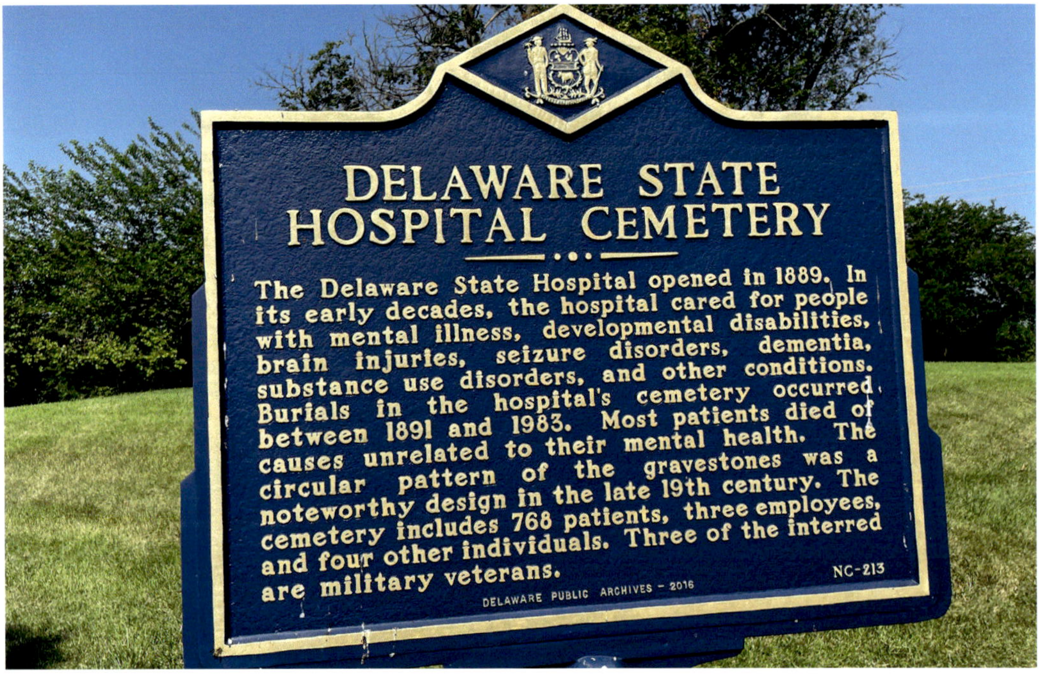

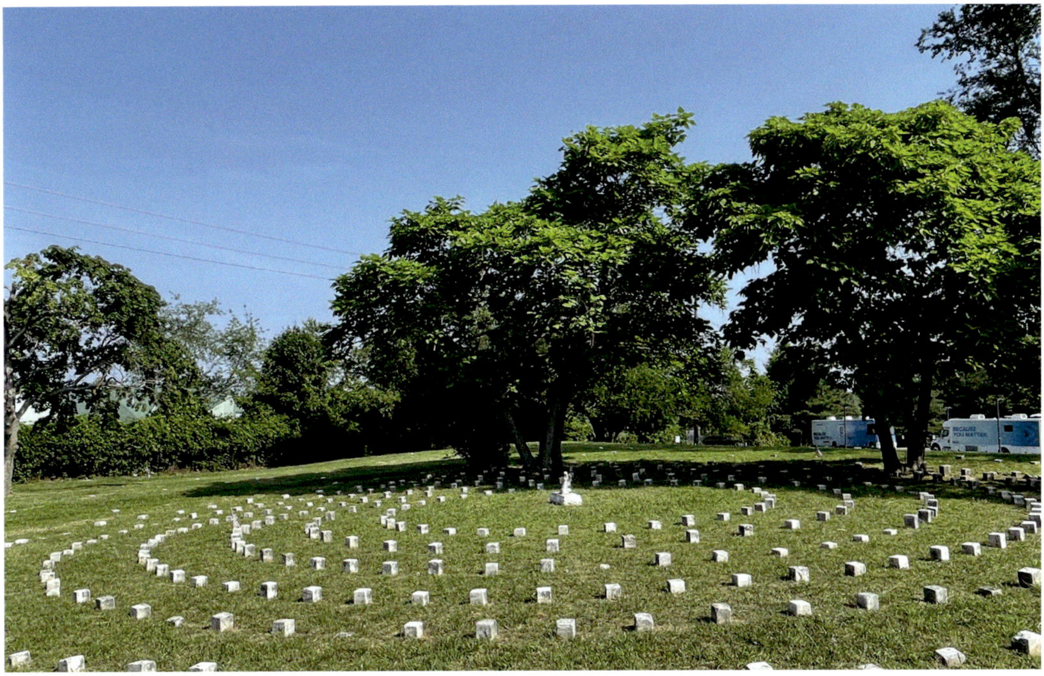

The rather unusual spiral burial pattern in the Delaware State Hospital Cemetery allowed for an ever-widening arc of new burials. Each stone is numbered, and records are kept of the interred.

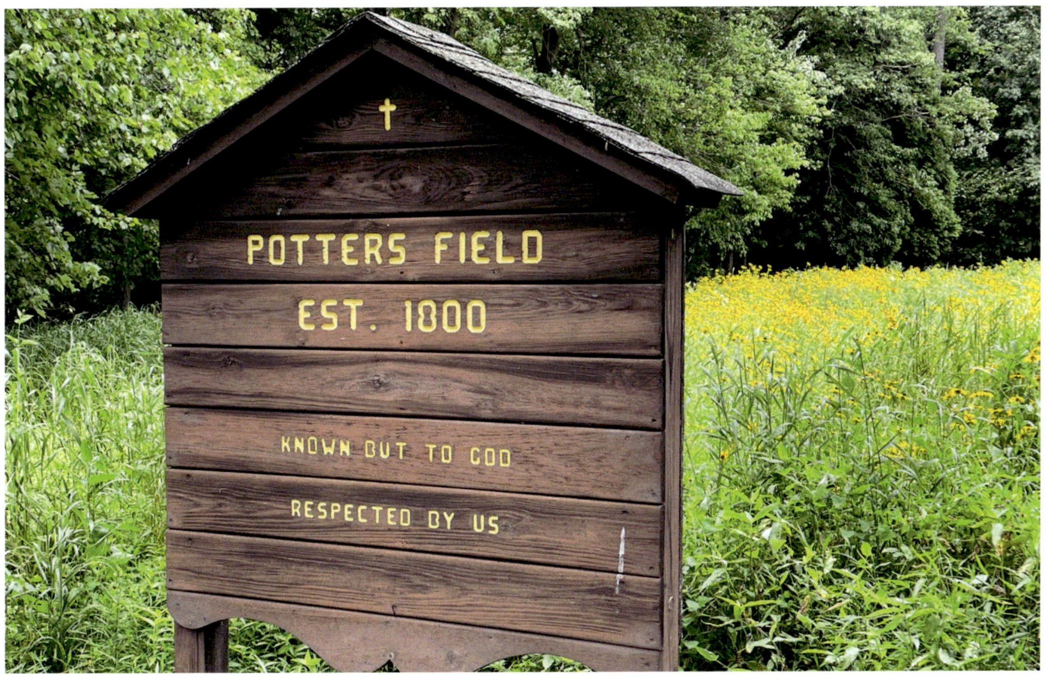

The Potters' Field at ChesLen Preserve in West Chester, PA, while having a lovely flower garden and signage, has no record of its burials. Hundreds of residents of the Chester County Poorhouse are buried there, including, some believe, "Indian" Hannah Freeman (1730–1802), the last Native American in Chester County, a member of the Lenni-Lenape tribe.

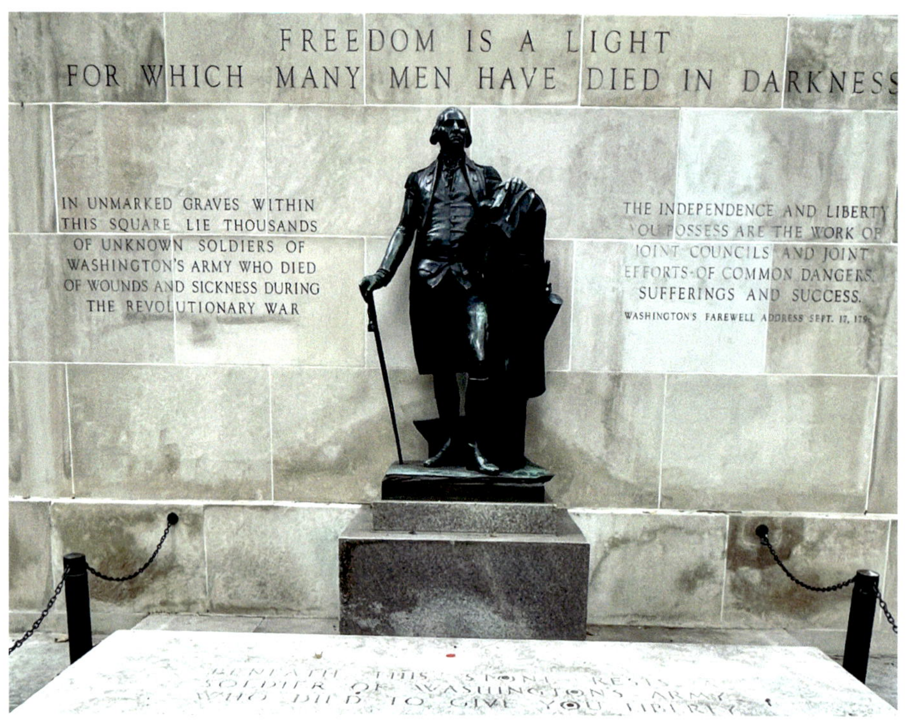

Washington Square Park at Seventh and Walnuts Streets, Philadelphia, had at one time been—and still is, technically—a mass grave for thousands of American and British Revolutionary War Soldiers. It was a Potters' Field before and after that. From 1706 until 1815 paupers, slaves, the friendless, criminals, strangers, and about 1,300 victims of the yellow fever epidemic were buried here.

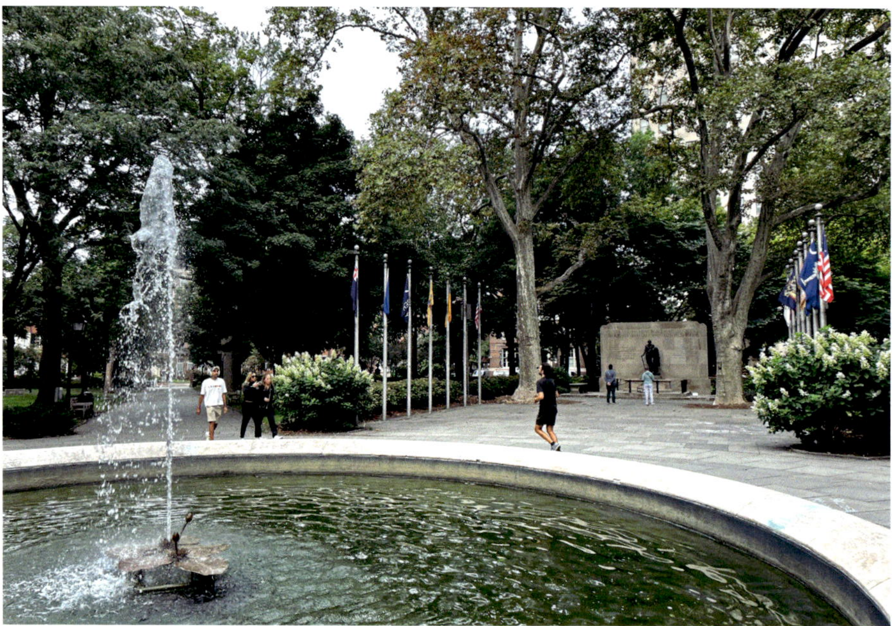

A popular stop on local ghost tours, Washington Square Park was a Potters' Field until 1815. Supposedly grave robbers used it to supply the Anatomy Department of nearby Jefferson Medical College with fresh cadavers. Cemetery guns with trip wires were supposedly installed to thwart the resurrectionists.

5

THE SURPRISE BELOW

The First Baptist Church of Philadelphia and Weccacoe Playground/Burial Ground

In 2016, workers were digging the foundation for a new condo high rise across from the Betsy Ross House at 218 Arch Street in Philadelphia's old city. They were greeted by the accidental exhumation of human bones. A tipster called the police. Perhaps unknown to the developer, this was the site of a very large old graveyard, the contents of which were supposedly relocated to the city's Mount Moriah Cemetery in 1860. The First Baptist Church of Philadelphia, founded in 1698, closed in 1855 and moved a few blocks away—leaving its graveyard behind.

The burial ground had been active from 1702 to 1859 and held an estimated 3,200 graves. It is now estimated that only about 150 bodies from the graveyard were relocated to the Mount Moriah plot purchased by the church. The majority, it seems, were simply abandoned, and built over. According to www.archstreetproject.org, from 1860 on, the site was a hat factory, a car repair shop, then most recently a parking lot.

After consultation with local archeologists, city officials said it could not intervene because the cemetery was inactive, and the land was private property. Although the developer was under no legal obligation to halt the work, it did allow Rutgers University, Camden, two weeks to get as many bodies out of the ground as it could in that time. They removed 160 full coffin burials.

The New York Times quoted Rutgers Professor and Director of Forensics Kimberlee Moran as having said, "there is a very characteristic 'pop' sound when a backhoe goes through a skull."[1] Excavation of the graveyard continued throughout the year by another archeological group. This ended in January 2018, after about 320 additional full coffins of skeletal remains had been removed. These were taken to a research facility where they were cleaned, analyzed, and, in some cases, even identified. Though no laws governed the situation, certain moral and ethical responsibility was exercised by many volunteers to excavate the remains so they could be reburied in Mount Moriah Cemetery, their planned destination. *The Philadelphia Inquirer* suggested that the excavation made apparent the need for stronger laws and proper enforcement concerning the disturbance of old unmarked burial grounds throughout Philadelphia.[2]

In 2024, the remains of these nearly 500 people that had been removed from the Arch Street site were reinterred in the First Baptist plot at Mount Moriah.[3] Why had only 150 bodies originally been moved to Mount Moriah in 1860? The City Health Office had only given the church four months, January to April 1860, to remove and relocate thousands of bodies. In the dead of winter, this may not have been physically possible. After the excavation in 2018, the estimated 2,500 remaining burials were built over. Obviously, the developer never saw the movie *Poltergeist*.

Weccacoe Playground in the Queen Village section of the city has a similar story, with 5,000 very quiet neighbors resting below the tennis courts and recreation center. As with so many Philadelphia sites where former cemeteries had existed, the property became something that did not require digging a foundation. When the Mother Bethel A.M.E. Church moved a few blocks away from this original location in 1889, it sold its graveyard to the city with the intent that the property would be used for a playground. The burial ground was paved over and forgotten about—until 2013, when it was rediscovered during a park improvement project.

Work stopped; experts were consulted. Neighbors were shocked to learn that under their playground and community center were the remains of over 5,000 Philadelphians—African American women, men, and children. In early America, Queen Village (Southwark, as it was called then) was home to a large free African American community. By 1820, 10,000 people lived in the neighborhood. The Bethel Burying Ground was established in 1810 by Mother Bethel A.M.E. Church and was possibly the first independent cemetery for African Americans in Philadelphia.[4]

What to do in a situation like this? Is it more respectful to move the bodies to another location or leave them be? It was decided to leave the bodies alone and work around them. In response to the rediscovery of the Bethel Burying Ground, an alliance was formed in 2013 to involve the church and educate the public about the site, protect it, provide historic designation, and develop a memorial. An historic marker was erected, and educational material attached to one side of the recreation center, which sits atop the graves.[5, 6]

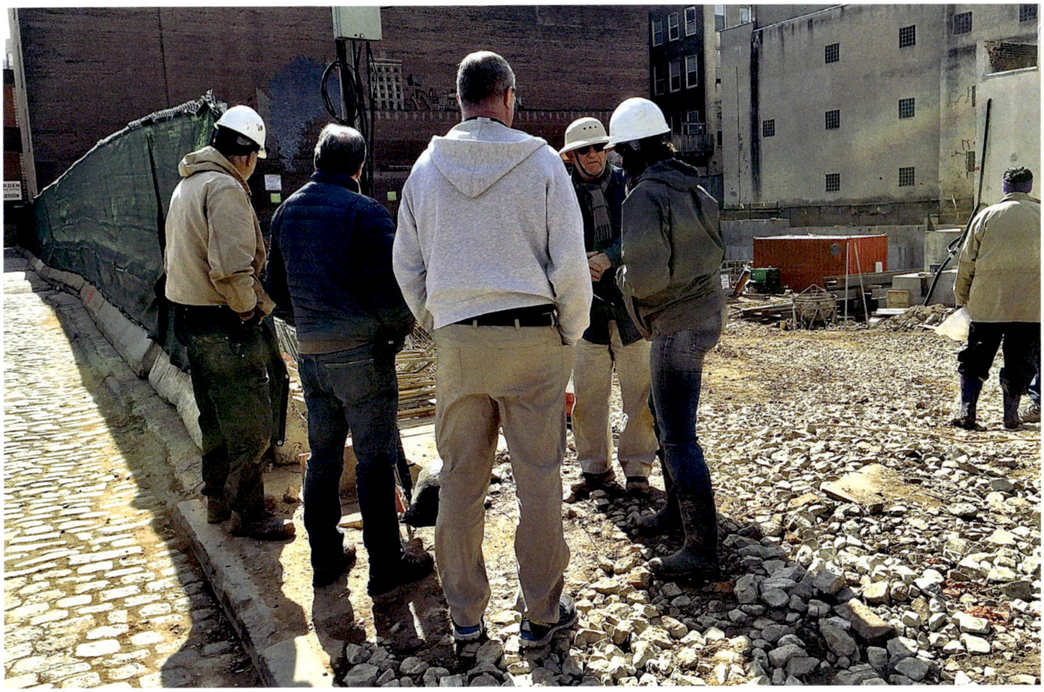

Work stopped in December 2016 when human bones surfaced in the construction dig at 218 Arch Street, Philadelphia. The area was soon recognized to be the 1702 First Baptist Church of Philadelphia Burial Ground.

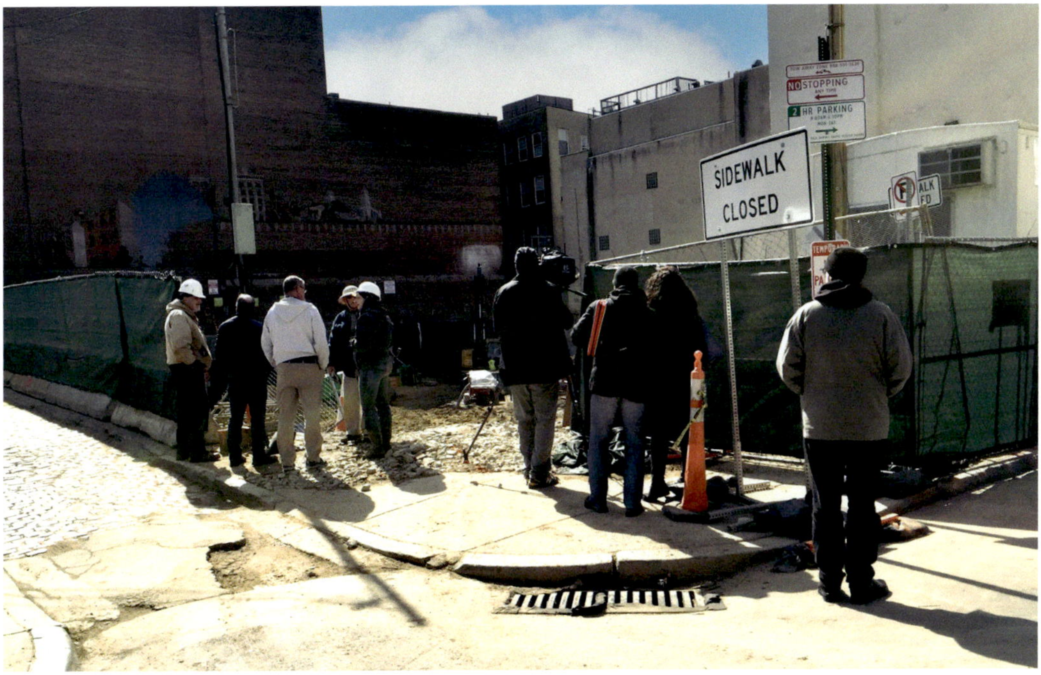

The City of Philadelphia did not intervene in the situation, as its Orphans' Court, which handles abandoned cemeteries, claimed it had no jurisdiction over the site due to it being private property.

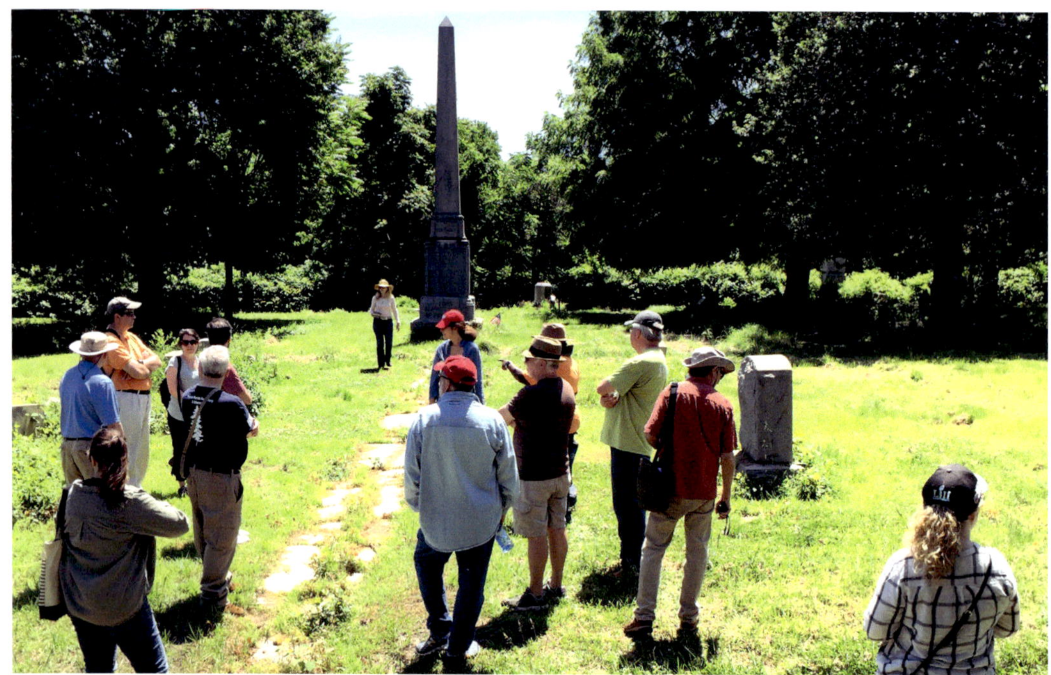

Only about 150 graves were relocated to the First Baptist Church burial plot at Mount Moriah Cemetery in 1860, with thousands left behind on Arch Street. The remains of approximately 500 people were moved from the Arch Street site in 2017 and reburied at the church's plot at Mount Moriah in 2024.

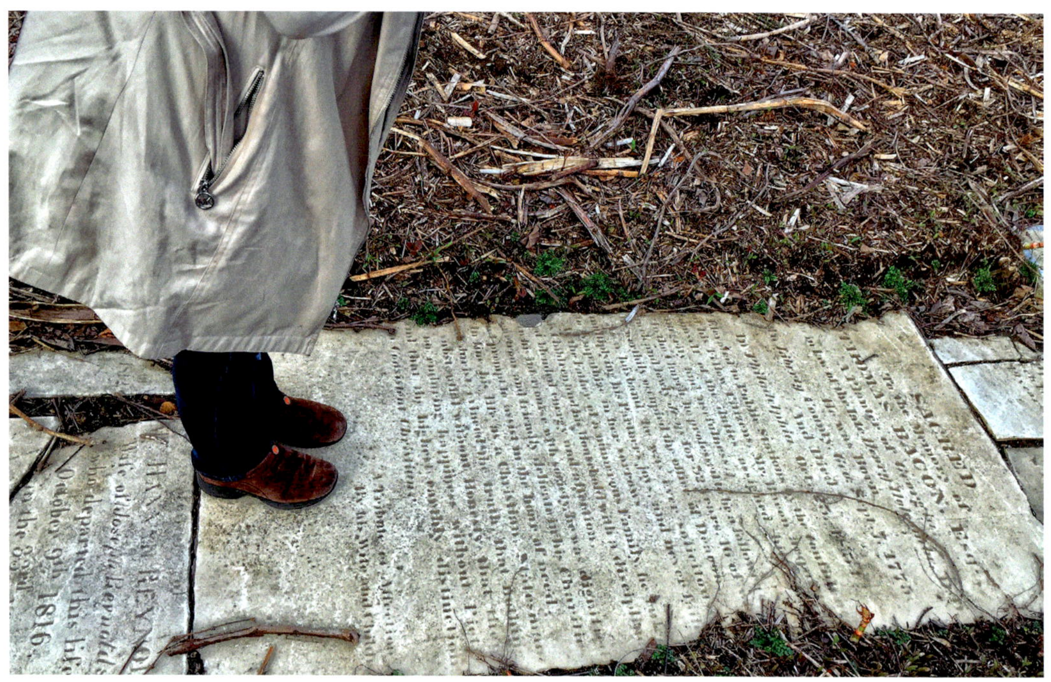

Oddly, a few grave markers from First Baptist Church Burial Ground were moved to the church's plot at Mount Moriah in 1860 and used as sidewalk pavers leading up to the central monument.

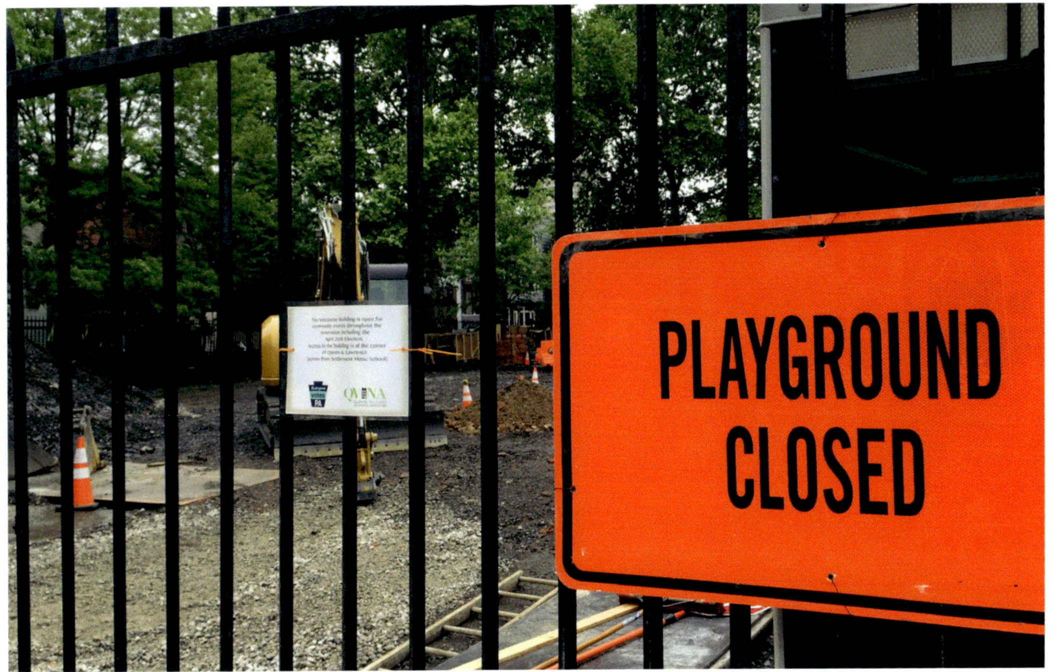

Weccaco playground in south Philadelphia was closed for renovations in 2013, and work was halted when burials and a gravestone were found beneath the asphalt surface. An estimated 5,000 burials from the Mother Bethel A.M.E. Church graveyard had been left behind when the church moved in 1889.

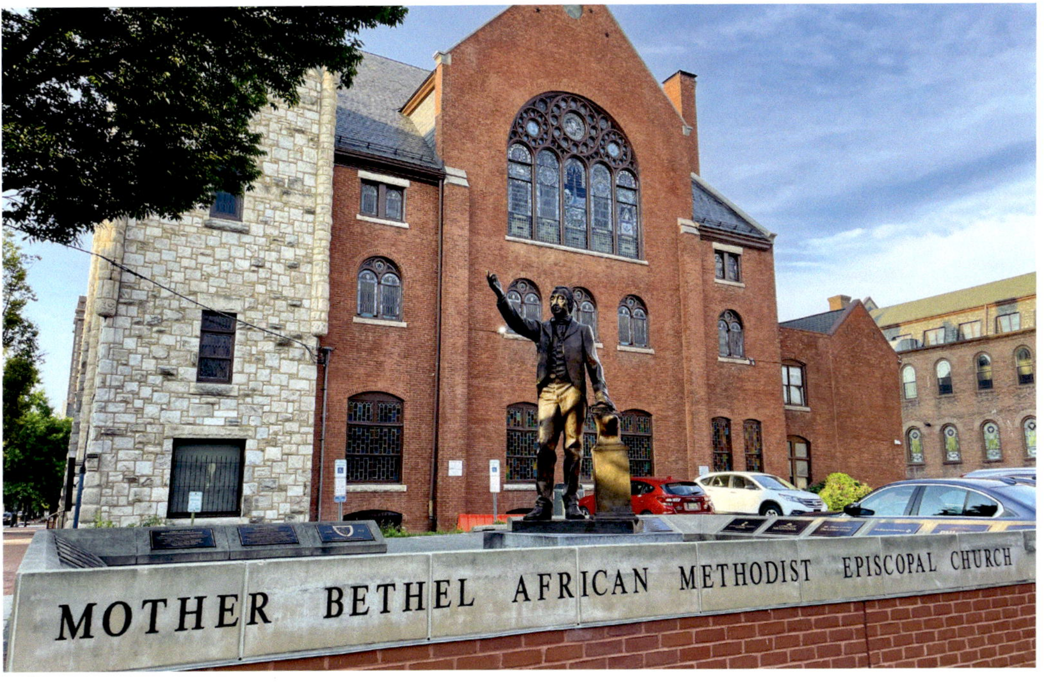

The Mother Bethel A.M.E. Church moved from the Weccacoe district to Sixth and Lombard Streets, a few blocks away. Shown is the church as it stands today. The burial ground was sold to the city with the clear intention it would be turned into a public park. Mother Bethel may have needed the funds to build the new church.

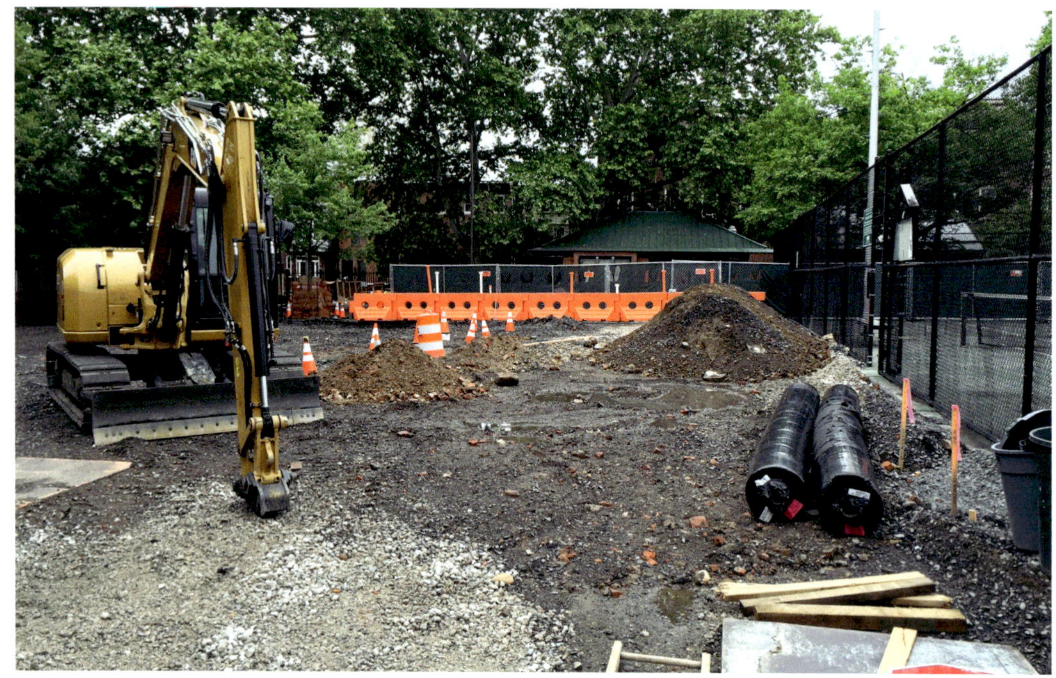

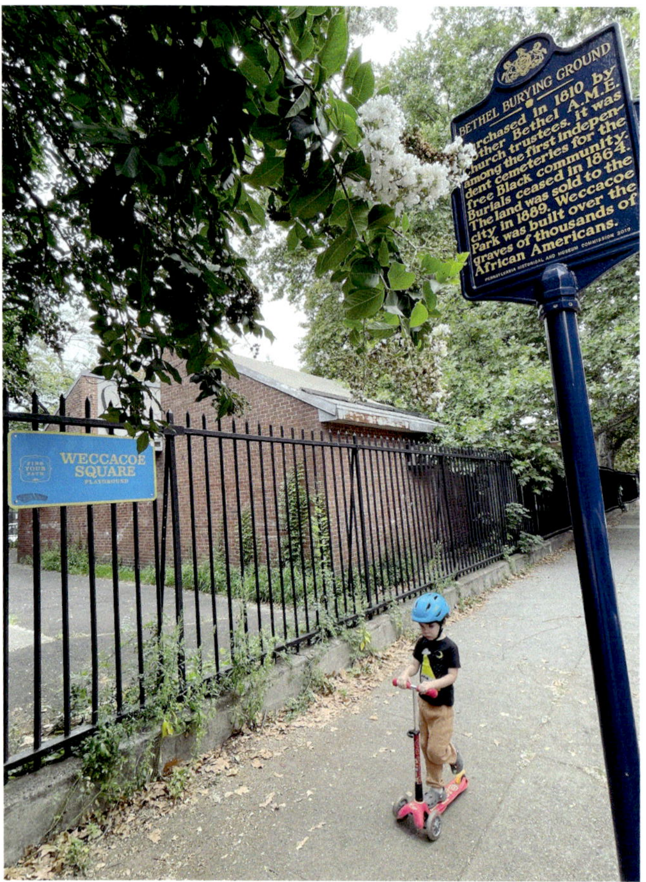

Above: After the boundaries of the burial ground were determined, work continued in Weccacoe Playground outside the burial area. An estimated 5,000 burials lie under the recreation center and tennis courts. Boundaries of the burial ground within the playground can be seen here: whyy.org/articles/sensitivity-and-the-search-for-common-ground-at-weccacoe-playground-bethel-burying-ground.

Left: Archeological exploratory excavations were done in 2014 to determine the depth and location of burials without disturbing or removing them. It was verified there were burials below the asphalt around the recreation center, as well as under the building itself and the tennis courts. These areas were refilled and new asphalt applied. Using ground-penetrating radar (GPR), the presence of intact coffins was detected in other areas of the park.

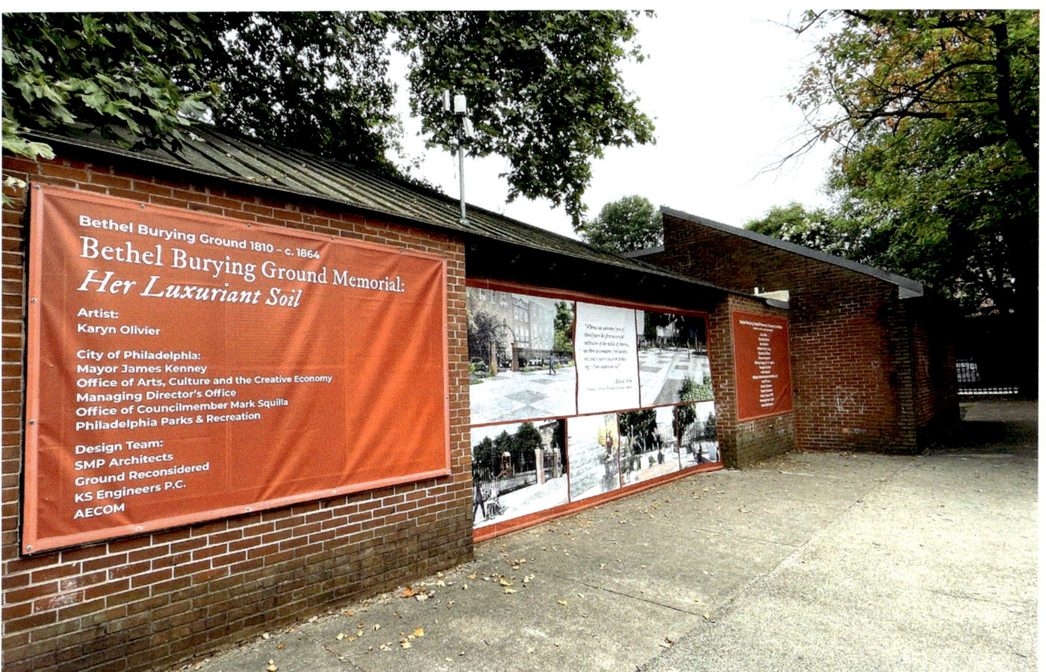

Above: After the renovations were completed and a spray park installed in 2016, informative banners were placed on the recreation center. Archeologists determined that burials began just 18 inches below the surface and continued down for many layers, with as many as nineteen grave shafts.

Right: Commemorating history while making room for the living is seen as a teachable moment for the children who use Weccacoe Playground.

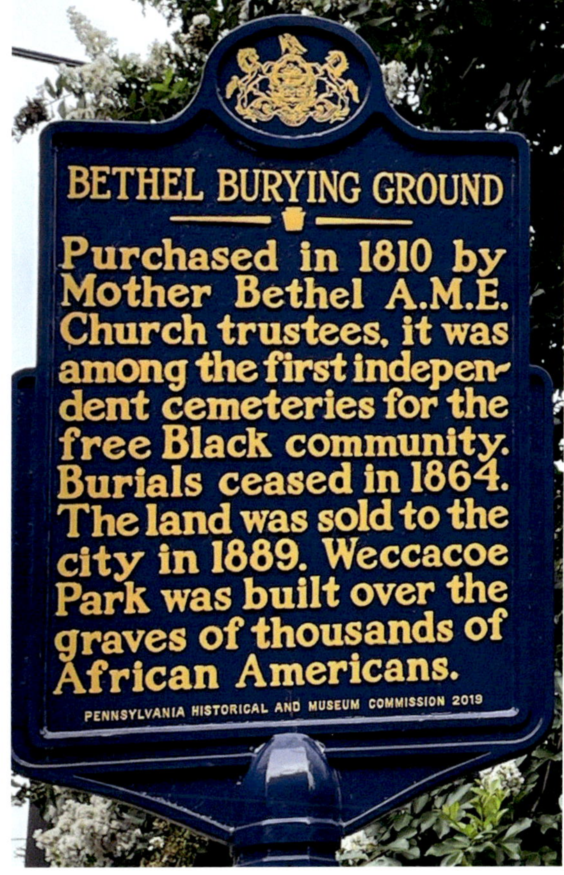

6

MOUNT MORIAH CEMETERY: A RESURRECTION

In 2011, Mount Moriah Cemetery was the largest abandoned cemetery in the nation—200 acres of overgrown forest. That is, except for the few acres that were being mowed by squatters. It is a very real possibility that the people who ran the operation in its later years were in no way connected to the owners who had died off along with the board of directors.

The people who placed themselves in charge mowed the grass and buried people in a specific portion of the cemetery. Most of the cemetery had grown dense with trees and weeds. The caretakers took money to bury people, set headstones, and keep records. Burials at Mount Moriah were reasonably priced and city residents routinely utilized these services. All seemed to be going well until 2010 when the operators became careless. Stones were not placed on graves in a timely manner, which eventually led to lawsuits. Knowing that they would soon be exposed, the people running the operation just left.

Weeds grew and covered the property. The gates were open and fencing was broken in many areas. All access invited all crime. The cemetery became such a frightening wasteland that families were afraid to visit. Access roads throughout the cemetery were overgrown and blocked by piles of refrigerators and wrecked cars.

Established in 1855, Mount Moriah is home to over 100,000 Philadelphians. Notables include Betsy Ross, the Bassett's Ice Cream founders, 1920s mobster Mickey Duffy, and William Barber (chief engraver for the U.S. Mint). Like Woodlands and Laurel Hill, this was a rural garden cemetery before the city grew around it. In the late 1800s, the grounds were covered with opulent grave markers, decorative plot border fencing, grand mausoleums, and Victorian birdhouses. What went wrong? Mismanagement of funds, theft, and lack of maintenance, most likely.

After being abandoned in 2010, most of its 200 acres grew into a vast woodland. It became a dumping ground, crime was rampant, and a marijuana farm grew in a clearing surrounded by high weeds. While it is easy to be judgmental about why the cemetery had been allowed to devolve to this sad state, it allows one to contemplate the results of human endeavor. Thankfully, many are invested in Mount Moriah as a living monument to Philadelphia's history.

In 2011, the volunteer group Friends of Mount Moriah Cemetery stepped in. With assistance from the City of Philadelphia, the group was devoted to stabilizing and maintaining the property. The city rounded up the wild dogs, cleared out the old cars and trash. The Friends were heavily dependent on volunteers and donations. Over time, word spread, and organizations sent busloads of volunteers to spend the day painting, raking, cutting invasive trees and loading them onto trucks.

The Friends of Mount Moriah Cemetery, Inc. became a 501(c)3 non-profit organization. Grants were applied for and awarded. The 1855 brownstone gatehouse was shored up, awaiting funds to preserve it. The office building was restored. Mowing equipment was purchased, landscapers contracted. Monument restoration companies volunteered their services to resurrect fallen monuments. Dedicated volunteers showed up every day with their riding mowers. Today, the cemetery gates are opened by volunteers each weekend for vehicular and pedestrian access. People picnic on the grounds, the way they did in Victorian times.

The tremendous effort put forth by literally thousands of people since 2011 has resulted in about 80 percent of the cemetery being taken back from nature. Invasive trees and poison ivy, knotweed and other foliage have been eradicated. Select trees are preserved and Mount Moriah is now a certified arboretum. Wreaths are placed on veterans' graves in December during the annual Wreaths Across America event. Bassetts' Ice Cream descendants distribute free ice cream on National Ice Cream Day.

Making this work difficult is the fact that old habits die hard. Occasionally the unguarded gates left open on weekends invite trucks looking for a place to dump trash. At one point there was a standoff between a full dump truck and the Friends President, Paulette Rhone (R.I.P.), who stood in front of the truck until it backed out of the cemetery. From the time it was abandoned in 2010, the cemetery has been maintained primarily through volunteer efforts organized by the Friends with assistance from the City of Philadelphia and Yeadon Borough (the cemetery is so large it spans two counties).

In 2014, the newly formed Mount Moriah Cemetery Preservation Corporation petitioned the court to dissolve the legacy (1855) Mount Moriah Cemetery Association and name the corporation as the receiver. As part of the argument as to why the receivership should be granted (with the goal that Mount Moriah would be saved from further deterioration), the attorney representing the corporation stated that the cemetery has 5,000 veterans, including twenty-three recipients of the Congressional Medal of Honor. In response, the judge made the pointed comment that all those buried at Mount Moriah deserve sanctity and respect, whether they have medals or not.

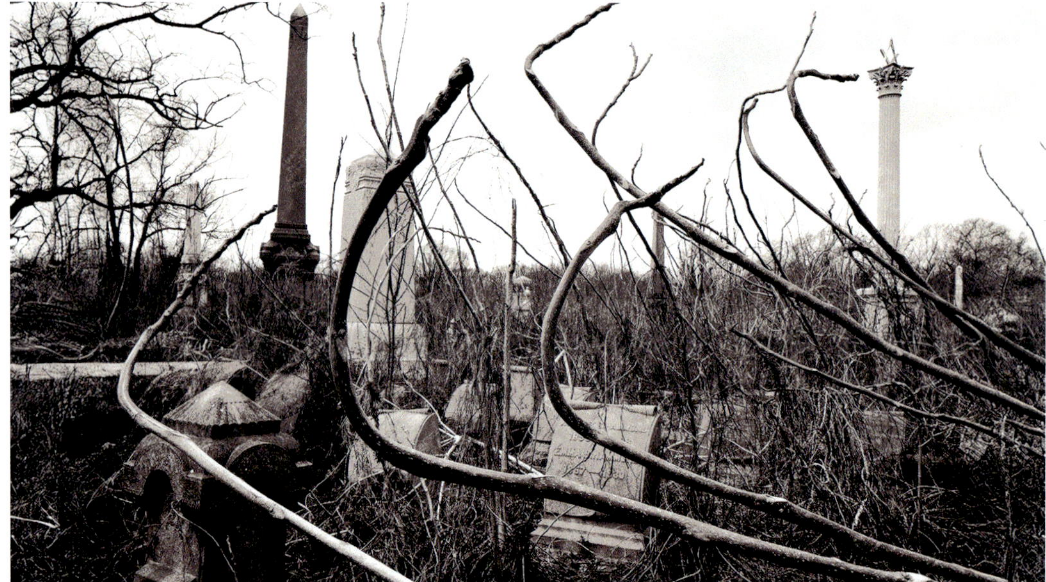

This dystopian scene was the Circle of Saint John in 2011, a large Masonic plot in Philadelphia's Mount Moriah Cemetery. After the cemetery was abandoned in 2011, the circle was unapproachable, surrounded by overgrowth whose thorns could pierce armor.

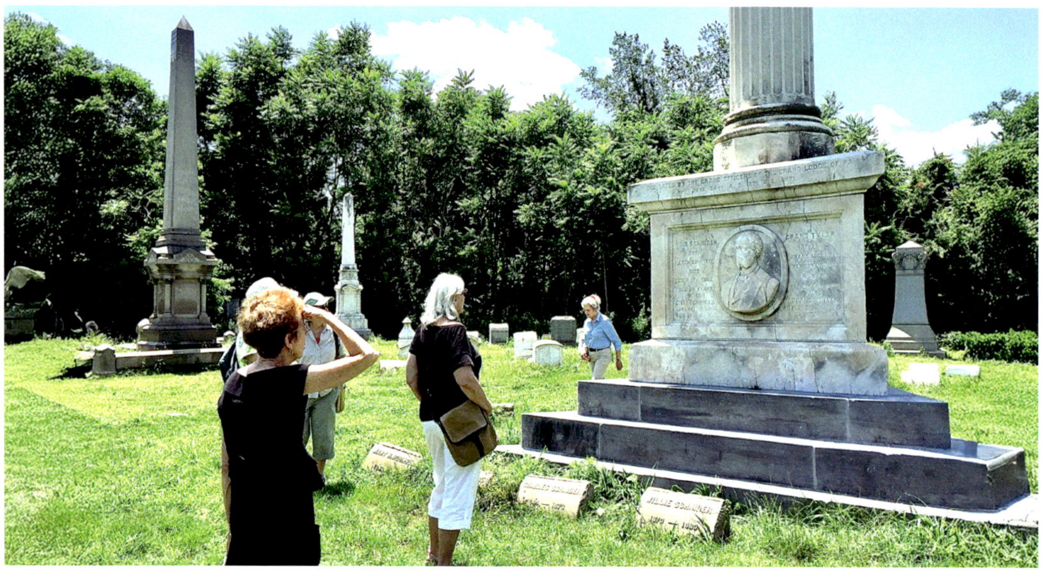

The central monument in the Circle of Saint John in a 2017 photo shows the difference that has been made by the Friends of Mount Moriah Cemetery, Inc. and countless volunteers.

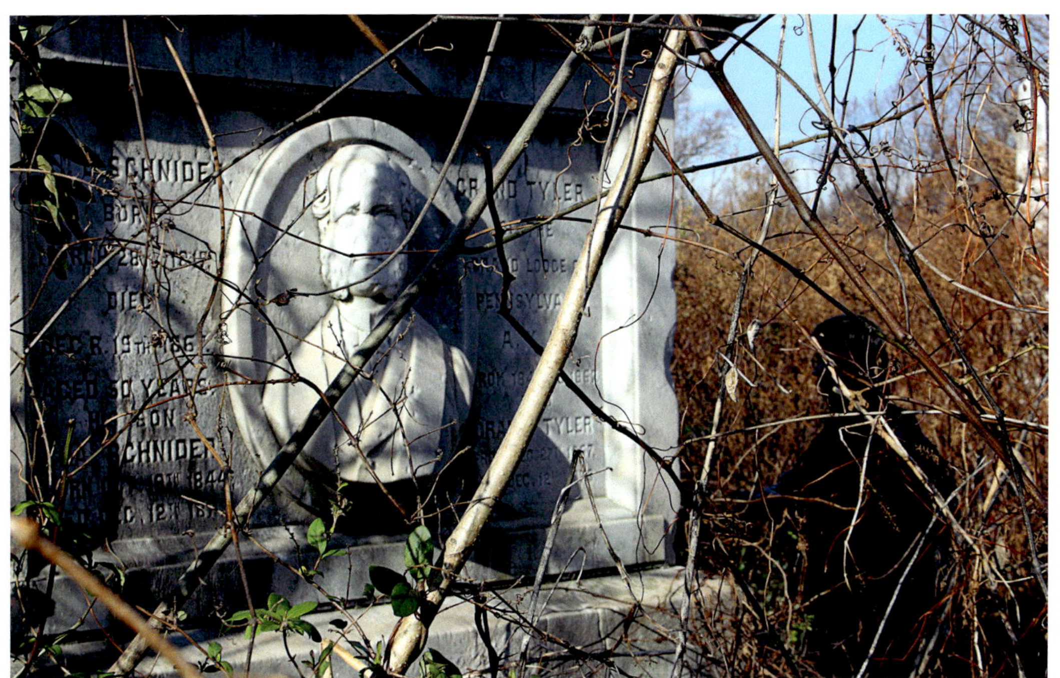

Above: A 2012 photo shows the central Grand Tyler monument in the Circle of Saint John. Masons from local lodges would periodically hack through the weeds with machetes and cut down encroaching trees with chainsaws to free a portion of the Masonic plot.

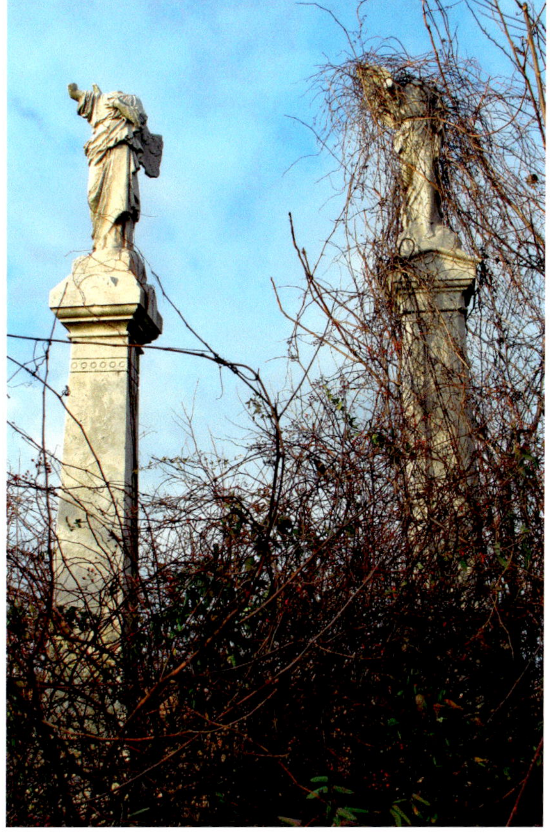

Right: Vandals, time, and weather erode efforts at immortality and the corruption of the cemetery seemed to affirm, rather than deny the decay below. Seeing it in this condition, you feel you are witnessing the final disappearance of the spirits of the dead. However, no condition is permanent.

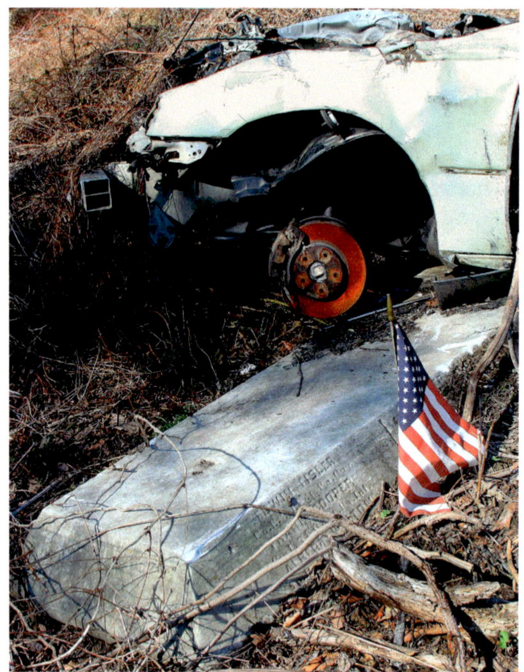

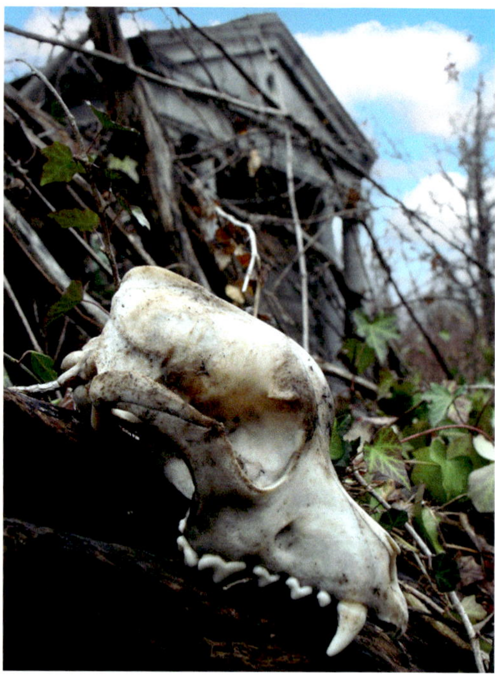

Above left: We erect monuments to the deceased for a purpose but attempts to preserve memories can sometimes be undermined.

Above right: Packs of wild dogs roamed the wilderness of Philadelphia's Mount Moriah Cemetery in the years after the cemetery was abandoned. The cemetery became such a frightening wasteland that geocache players hid their boxes out behind mausoleum hill, where criminals dumped the dead bodies from dogfights.

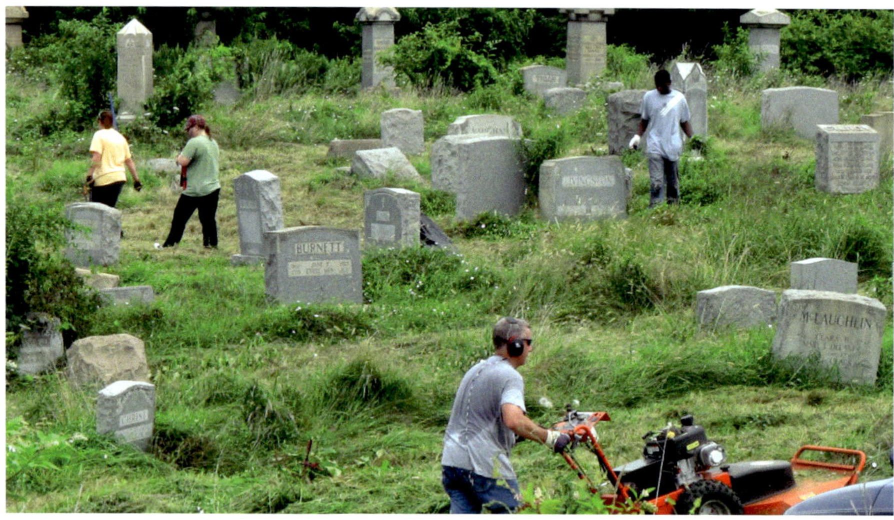

Beginning in 2011, volunteers brought their own lawnmowers and weed whackers to tame the wild weed growth in select areas of Mount Moriah. As more ground was taken back from nature, more volunteers arrived to broaden the scope of the massive landscaping program developed by the Friends of Mount Moriah Cemetery, Inc. Organized by the Friends, volunteer cleanups sponsored by the civic engagement programs of various colleges and businesses continue from spring through fall.

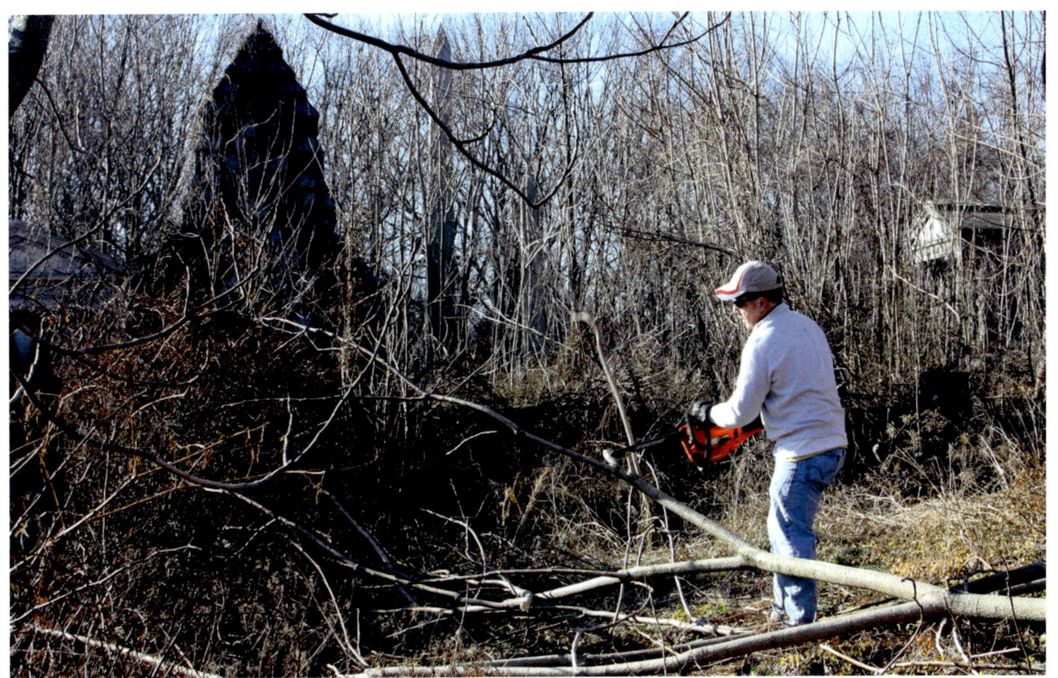

For a few years, it was a chainsaw paradise—one of the few abandoned cemeteries where you did not have to be afraid if you heard a chainsaw revving up behind you. Mausoleum Hill on the Yeadon, PA side of the cemetery was so dense with trees and overgrowth, the mausoleums could not be seen in the green of summer.

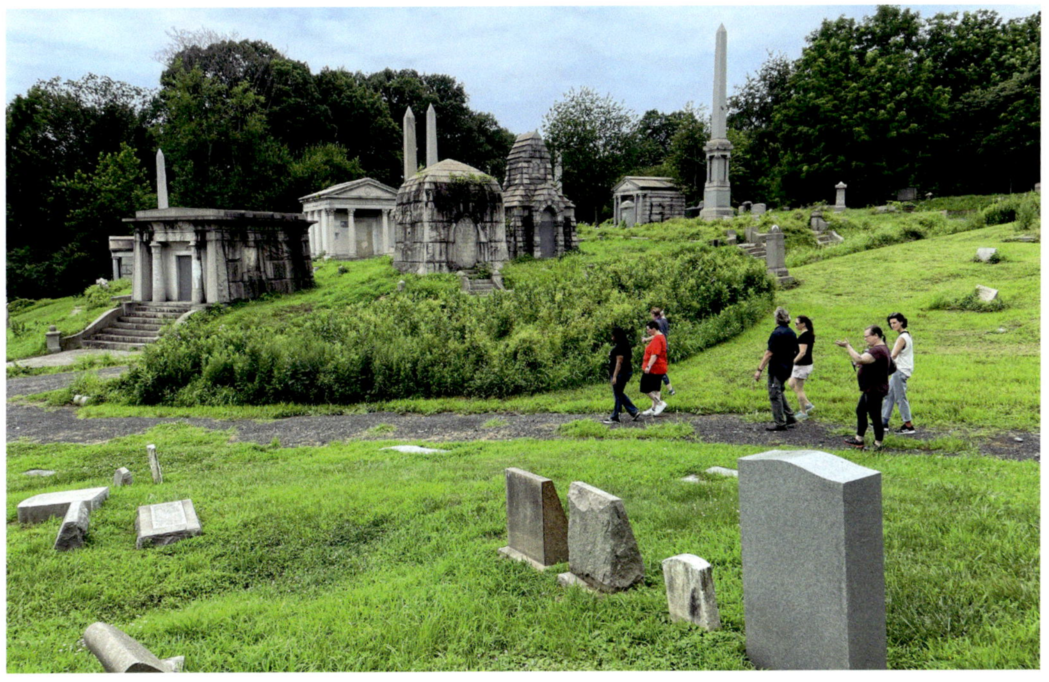

Currently, Mausoleum Hill is kept well-maintained. Since 2011, the Friends have organized events with thousands of volunteers who have participated in cleanups, planting, grave location, genealogical research, and historic tours. As the size of Mount Moriah is over 200 acres, the work is challenging.

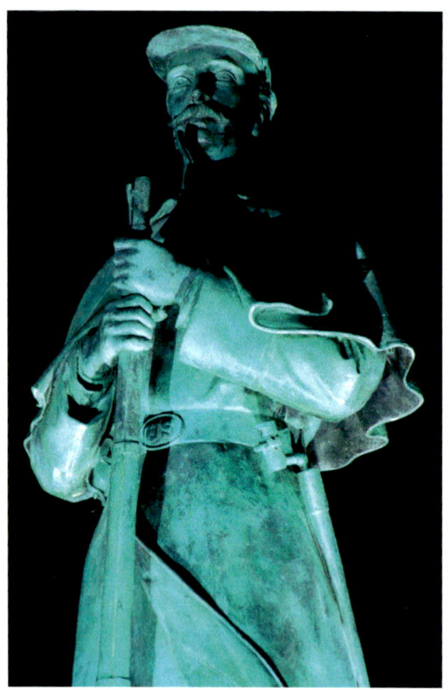

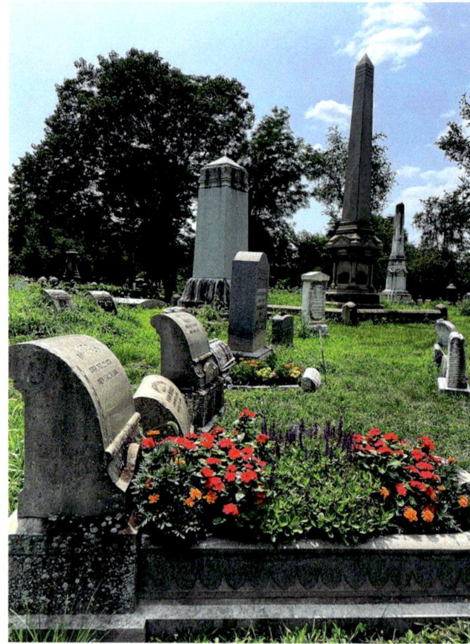

Above left: Due to scrap metal drives that aided the war effort, most of the metal in the cemetery disappeared during WWII. The bronze Civil War soldier statue, "The Silent Sentry," was nearly stolen—chained and dragged out of the cemetery. It was rescued and installed temporarily at Laurel Hill Cemetery, where it stands today.

Above right: Gardeners renew the Victorian practice of planting flowers in cradle graves. This was the original intent of "cradle" graves—they do not necessarily imply an infant's grave.

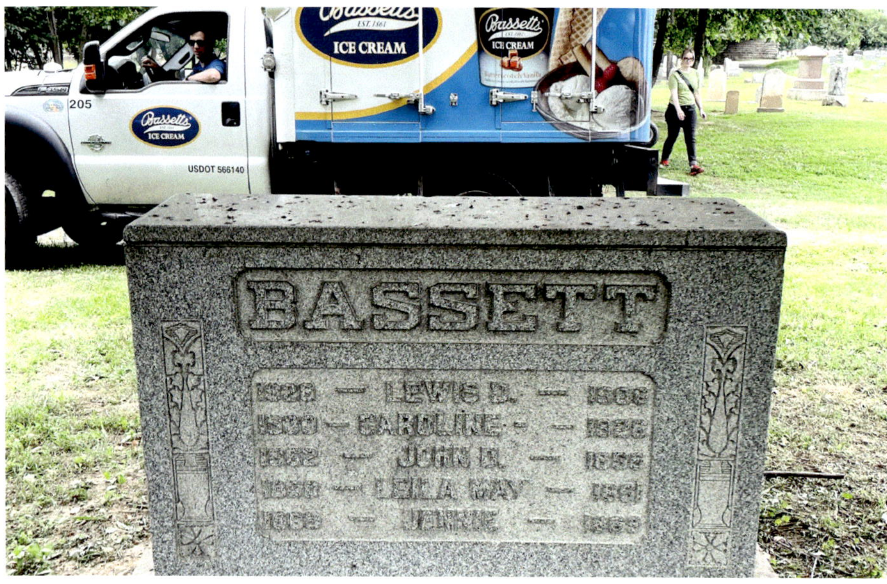

Bassetts' Ice Cream company descendants distribute free ice cream on National Ice Cream Day, the third Sunday in July. The Bassetts company founder Lewis Dubois Bassett, buried at Mount Moriah, was the first tenant to sign a lease in the newly opened Reading Terminal Market in 1893. The stand is still in the market, with the original marble countertop.

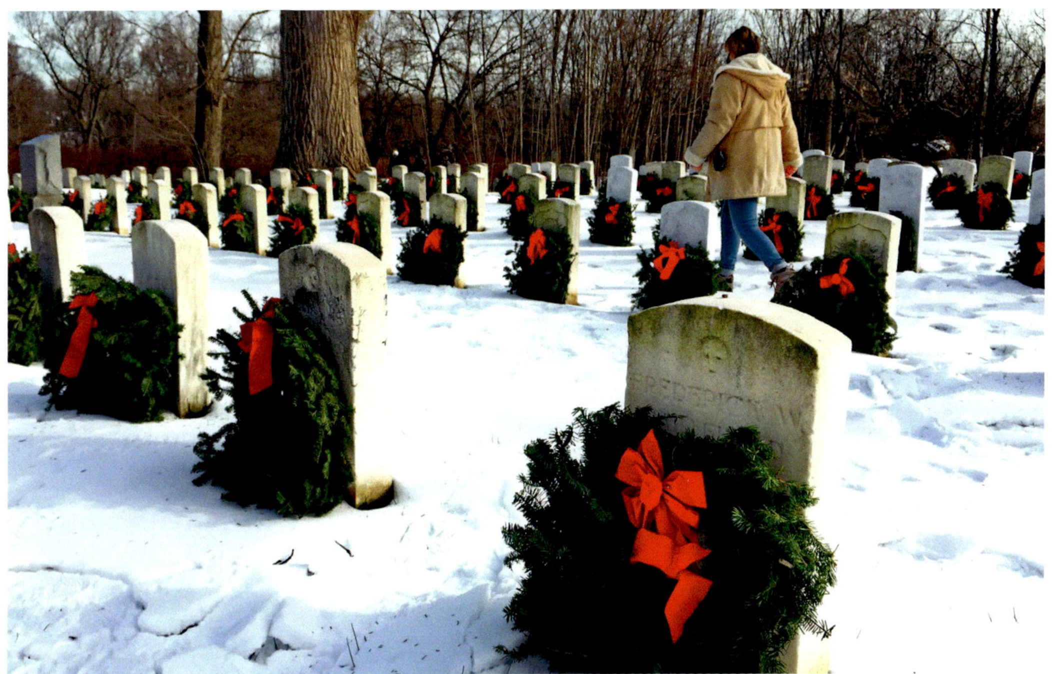

Wreaths are laid on graves in the U.S. Naval Asylum plot and Civil War Soldiers plot in Philadelphia's Mount Moriah Cemetery. National "Wreaths Across America" day is a volunteer program of donating money and laying wreaths on graves each December to remember those who served in the U.S. military (www.wreathsacrossamerica.org). The event is sponsored annually by the Friends of Mount Moriah Cemetery, Inc.

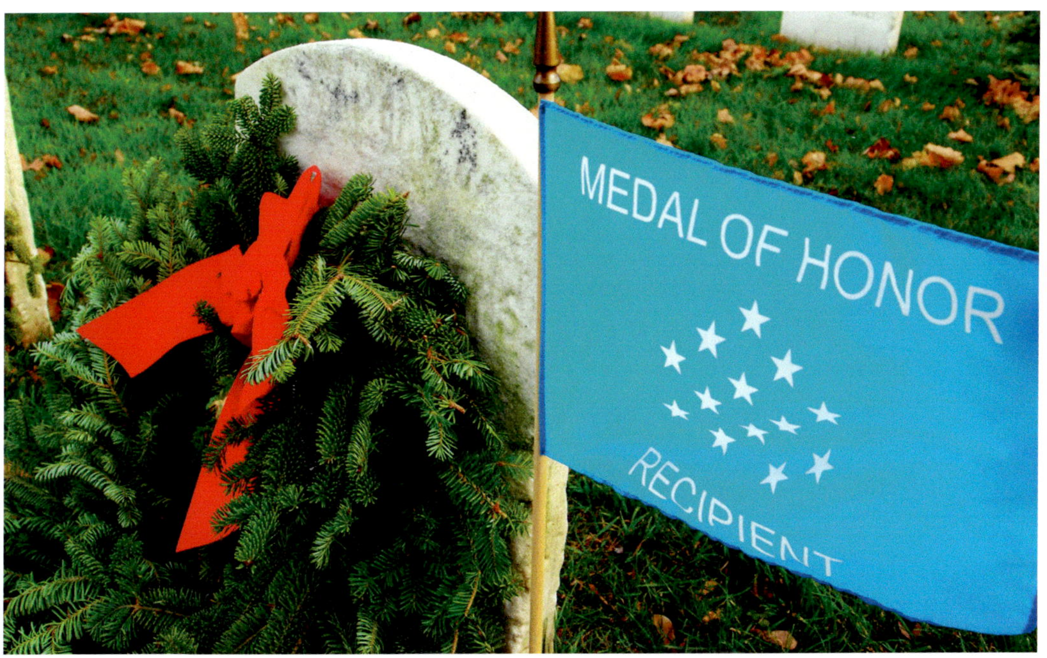

Within two Veterans' Administration National Cemetery plots at Mount Moriah, 5,000 veterans repose, including twenty-three recipients of the Congressional Medal of Honor.

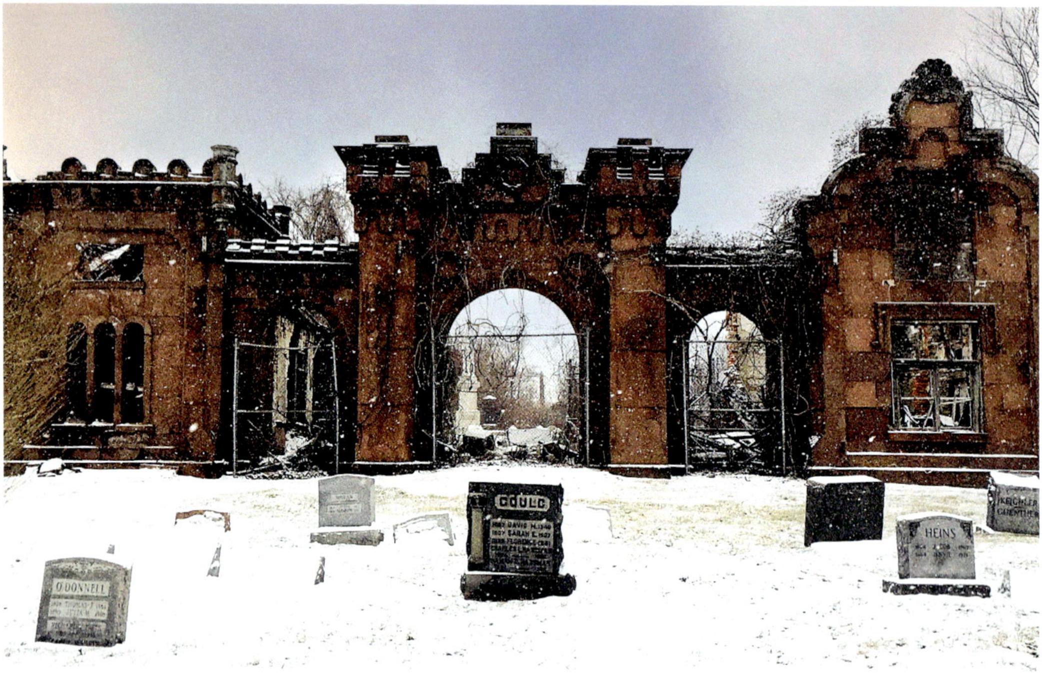

Mount Moriah's 1855 gatehouse was designed by architect Stephen Decatur Button, who also designed the gatehouses at the pre-Civil War Evergreen Cemetery in Gettysburg, the Colestown Cemetery in Cherry Hill, New Jersey, and the Odd Fellows' Cemetery in Philadelphia.

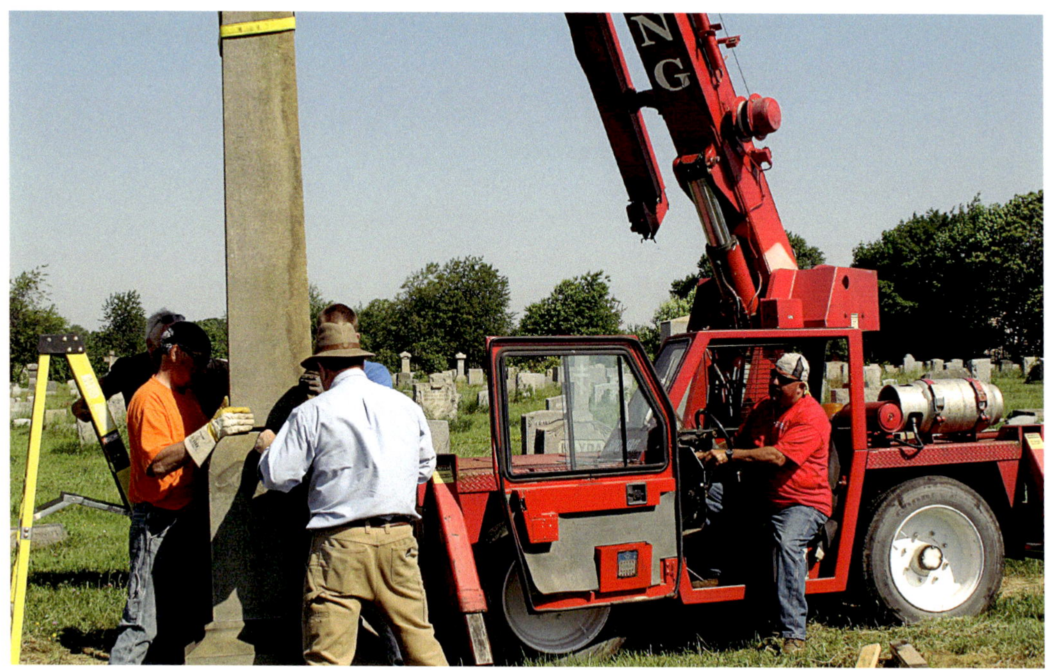

Monument reassembly at Mount Moriah Cemetery would not be possible without companies like Kreilick Conservation, LLC (Oreland, PA) volunteering their time, equipment, labor, and specialized knowledge. Fallen monuments can occur when the ground subsides or shifts over time. This is one reason people are warned about climbing on or leaning against headstones or any stone memorial in a cemetery.

Contrary to popular belief, Betsy Ross is not buried at the Betsy Ross House in Philadelphia's old city. She rests here under the thirteen-star flag at Mount Moriah Cemetery. The city attempted to move her grave for the nation's bicentennial in 1976 but could not excavate any remains from this location.

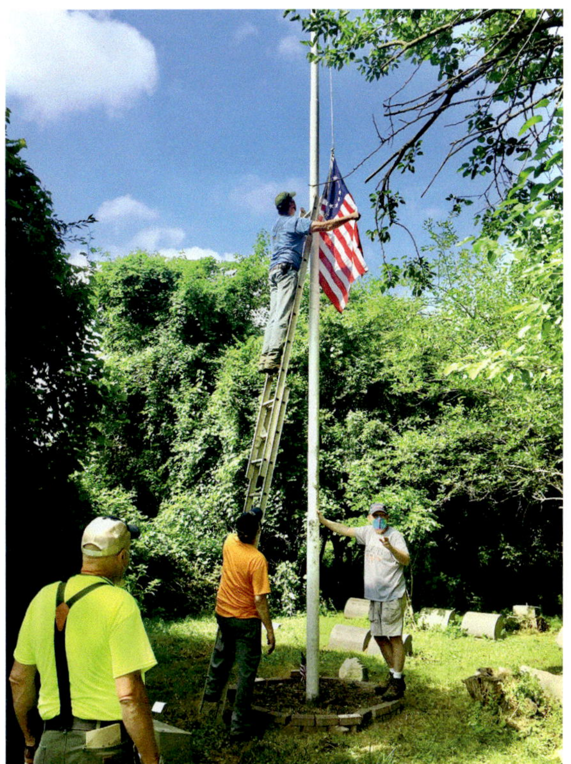

As of 2024, about 25 percent of Mount Moriah's 200 acres are still wooded. Some areas will be left in their natural state, after any invasive species have been removed. This natural habitat is populated with deer, fox, hawks, and other wildlife. Around 2015, an archery hunter who bagged a deer on the property was scared away by two female volunteers holding running chain saws. Over time, video surveillance has helped reduce illegal activity.

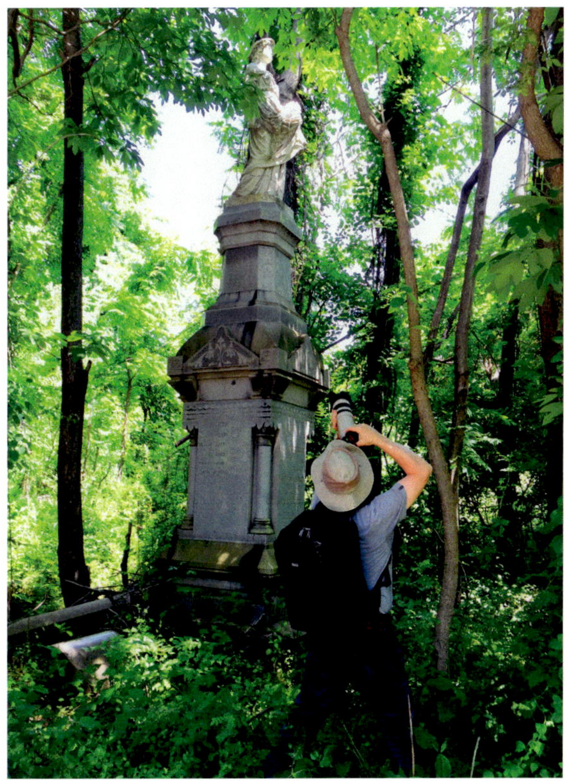

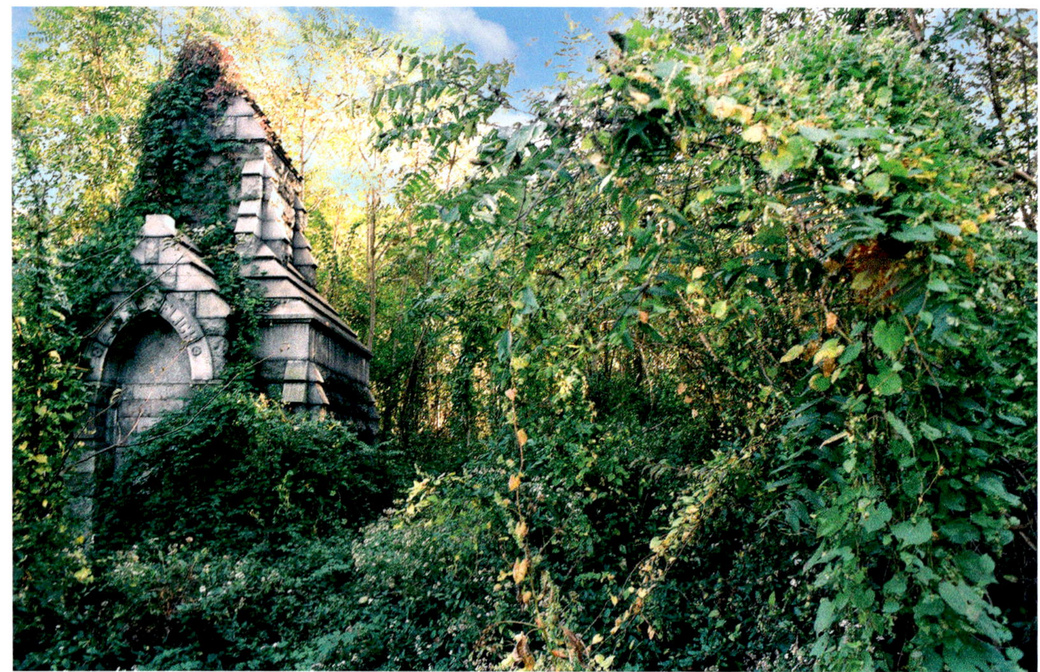

In the early days of rampant overgrowth on Mount Moriah Cemetery's Mausoleum Hill, even the most intrepid urban explorers backed away when they found themselves being tracked by wild dogs or came upon a coil of rope in the woods with a bag of lye nearby.

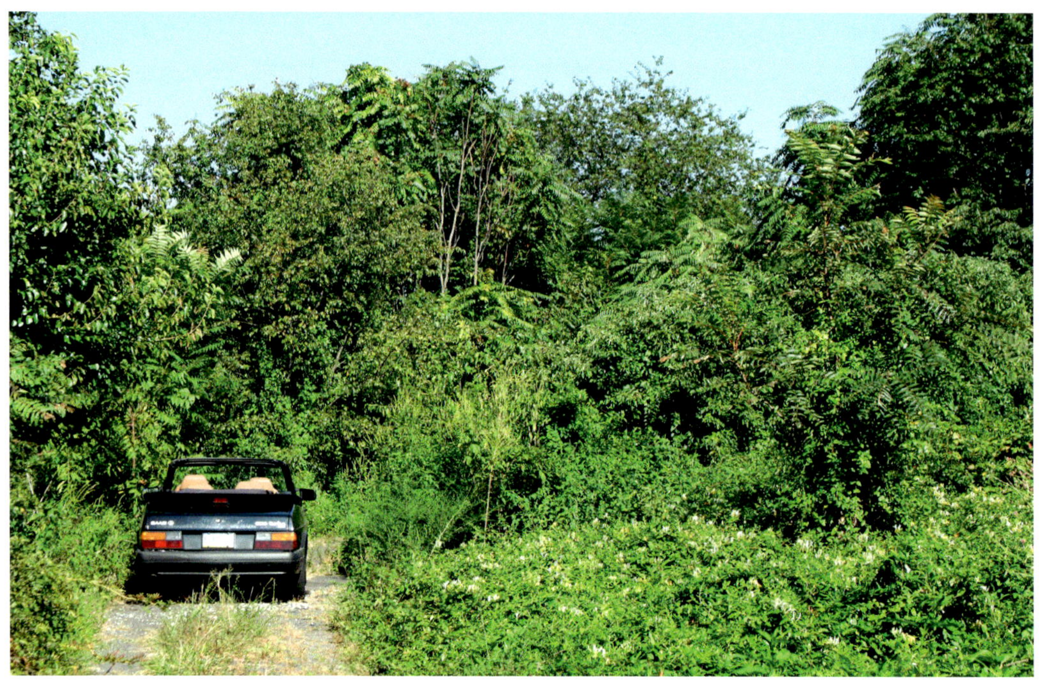

In 2008, most of Mount Moriah was overgrown except for select areas where burials continued. Roads throughout the cemetery were blocked by trees, piles of old tires, burned-out cars, or discarded building materials.

7

THE CEMETERY BUSINESS MODEL, OLD AND NEW

As America grew, so did its cemeteries. The town's common burial ground and church graveyards filled up. Relocating burial grounds outside the town or city, i.e., the rural cemetery movement, was a result of the waves of yellow and scarlet fever epidemics in the late 1790s. Joy Giguere states that New Haven, Connecticut, addressed this issue with the design of its New Burying Ground in 1796.[1] The novel design created a template for urban burial space reform that was quickly adopted elsewhere. It incorporated a rural location, large space, and intentional design elements that created a site for mourning, leisure, and interaction with nature. From this template evolved the Victorian garden cemeteries like Laurel Hill in Philadelphia (1836).

Ironically, New Haven's rural cemetery emphasis on creating a space for both solitude and recreation in a natural setting has in many ways become the saving grace of many of these historic (and now full) cemeteries. It appears that these very same attributes are again drawing the public to these green spaces.

Victorian-era cemeteries that survived into the year 2000 were faced with immense financial challenges. Many were full, so there was no burial income. It is rare that a cemetery can easily expand beyond its original boundaries to bury more people. Trust funds that had been set up 100 years ago barely provide enough interest income to keep the grass cut. If a full cemetery chooses to stay in business and has no philanthropic funding source, it needs to creatively expand its services beyond the traditional burial. Erecting a columbarium for cremains, charging to bury cremains, allowing green burials, even deathcare for pets can all result in needed revenue.

The year 2000 became a turning point in the Philadelphia area, with a resurgence of interest in these green spaces. People began to visit cemeteries. Woodlands Cemetery in West Philadelphia noticed that more local residents began to jog and walk their dogs on the property. That led to organized activities of all kinds on the grounds—everything from gardening in the cradle graves to runners' events and night tours (donations welcome). Holy Redeemer Cemetery in Philadelphia's Bridesburg neighborhood leaves all the gates of its 20-acre cemetery open on evenings and weekends for neighbors to stroll and for children to ride bikes.

The year 2020 was another turning point in the upswing in cemetery popularity across the nation. Why? The COVID-19 pandemic forced people to stay indoors away from others. If they went outside, they needed to avoid crowded spaces. National Parks became more popular than ever. The cemetery was the largest walkable open space in town. The pandemic focused peoples' attention on the value of these accessible green spaces.

It is unlikely that cemeteries will resort to charging admission, the way some did in Victorian times. However, many cemeteries are doing all they can to draw people in with a wide variety of cultural and social programming and sometimes an admission fee is charged. Mount Moriah Cemetery hosts historic tours, and an annual fall event called Darksome Art and Craft Market, which draws thousands of people.[2] Laurel Hill Cemetery offers Civil War reenactments, a classic hearse show, even a Halloween concert where the punk band The Dead Milkmen rock the receiving vault—and people are dying to get in! The income helps support the cemeteries and their upkeep, which includes cutting the grass, plowing snow, security, and raising fallen monuments.

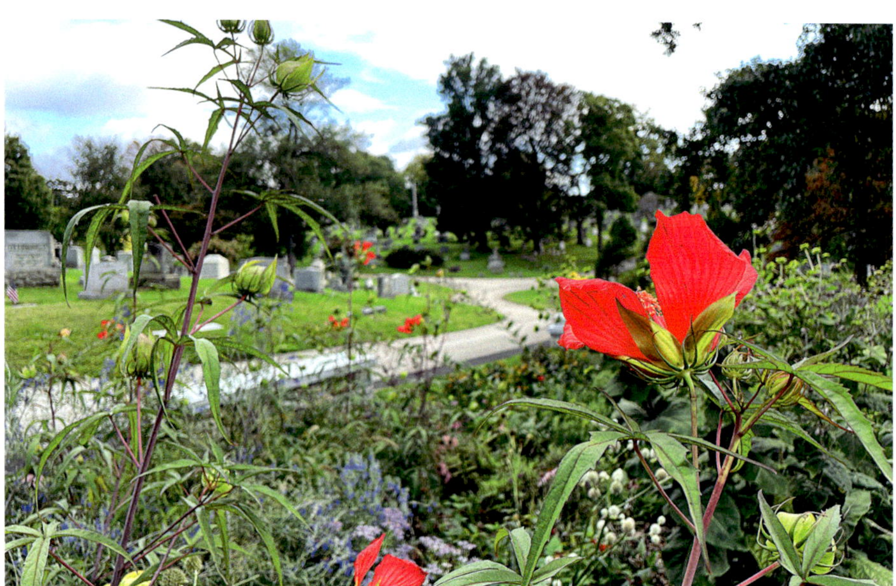

Green burial garden, West Laurel Hill Cemetery, Bala Cynwyd, PA (the sister cemetery to historic Laurel Hill Cemetery, Philadelphia). In 2008, "Nature's Sanctuary" at West Laurel Hill was the first natural burial ground in the Philadelphia area to be certified by the Green Burial Council (www.greenburialcouncil.org).

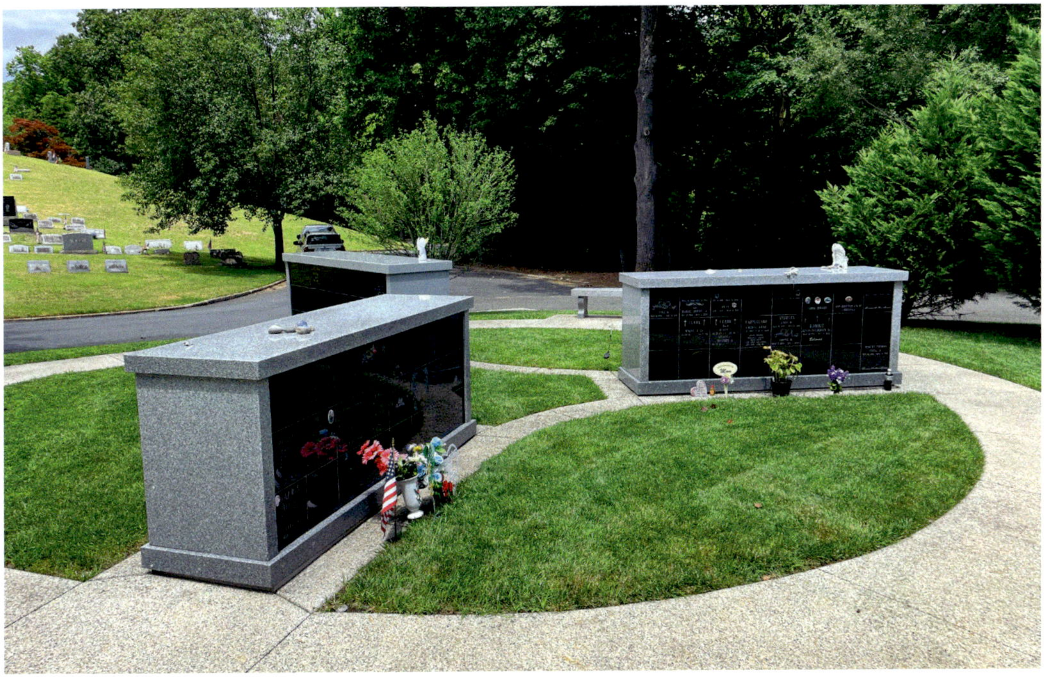

Columbarium with niches for cremains (usually in a cremation urn) have recently been installed at Wenonah Cemetery, Wenonah, New Jersey.

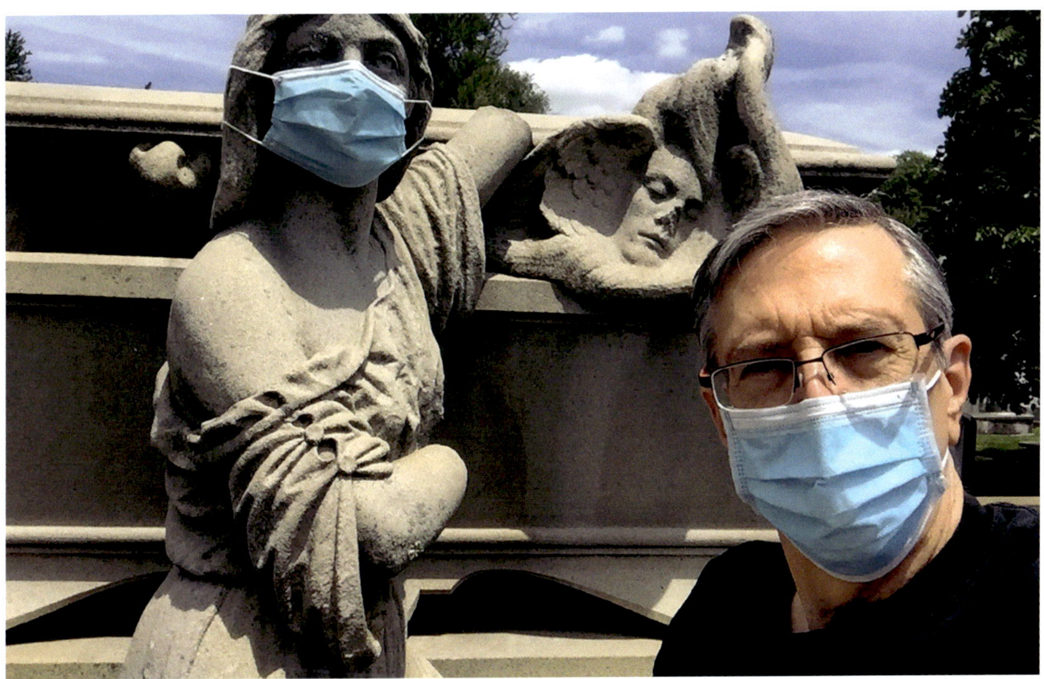

Laurel Hill Cemetery was one of many Philadelphia area cemeteries that saw a huge upswing in foot traffic during the COVID-19 pandemic. Visitors could easily maintain the 6-foot social distance rule as everyone they came into contact with was 6 feet under!

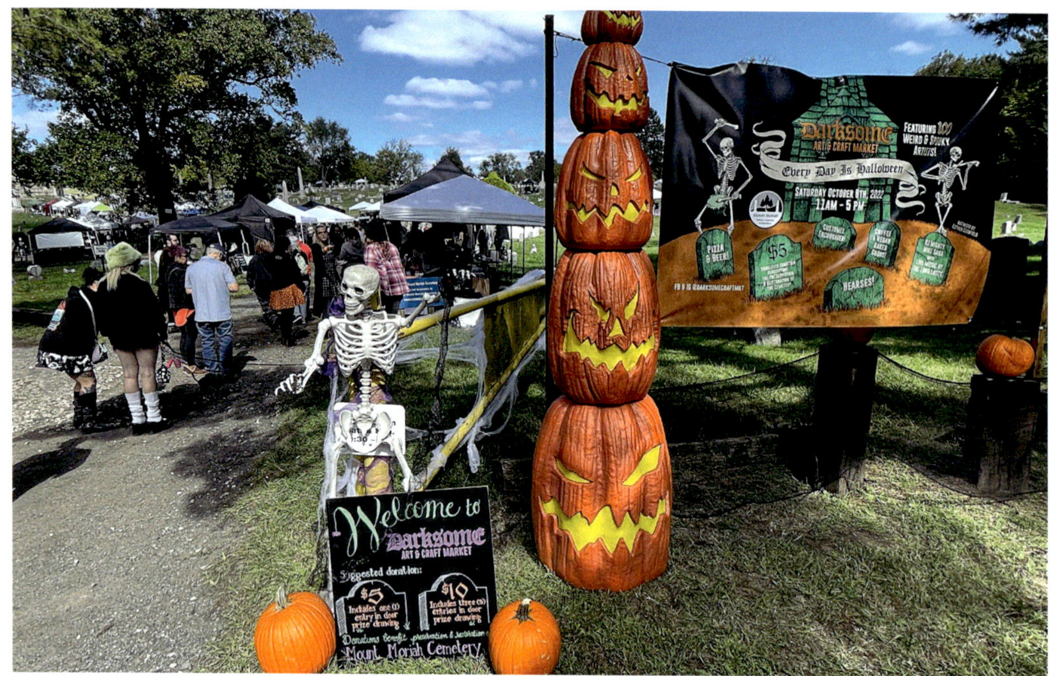

The Darksome Art and Craft Market (www.darksomecraftmarket.com) is hosted by Mount Moriah Cemetery each fall. Donations to Mount Moriah always welcome! (*friendsofmountmoriahcemetery.org/support*)

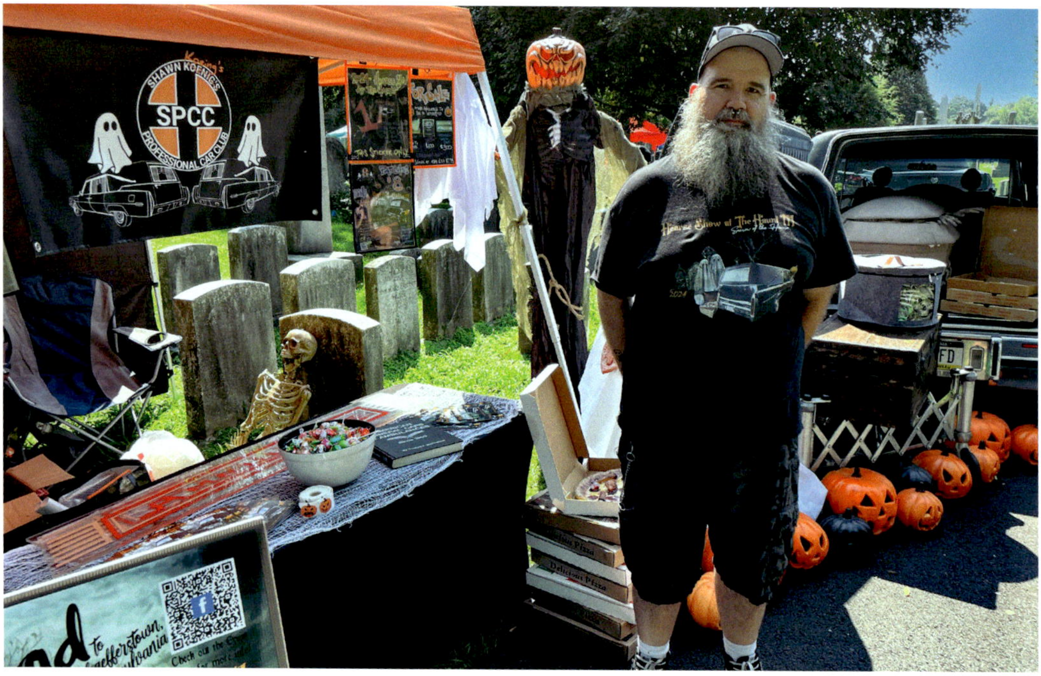

Classic hearse shows are hosted by Laurel Hill Cemetery, Philadelphia, throughout the year. This is one of many fundraising and community engagement events the cemetery offers.

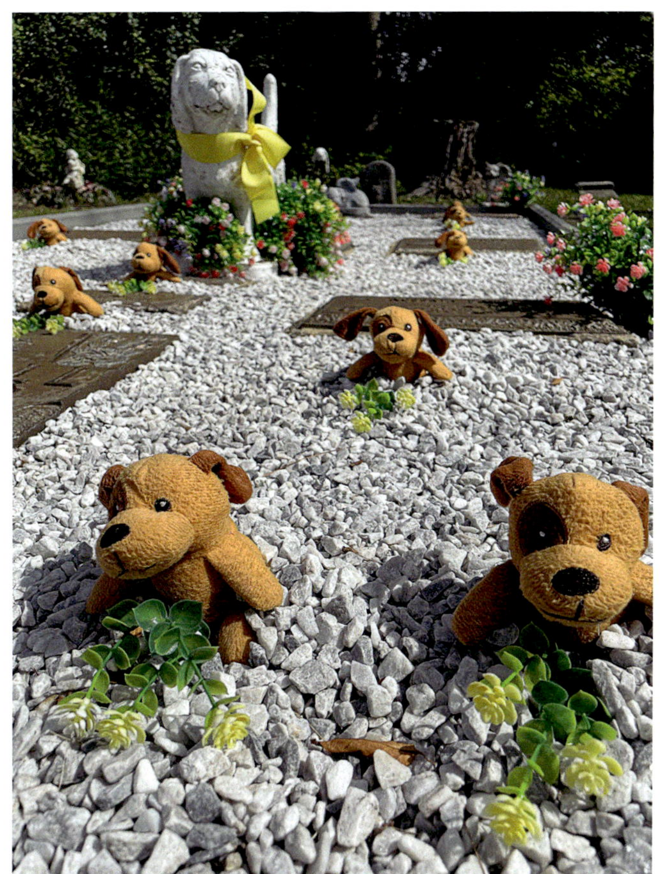

Right: Pet death care and burials are one way that traditional cemeteries are generating much-needed revenue.

Below: Vendors at Laurel Hill Cemetery's annual Market of the Macabre offer death-related arts and crafts including jewelry, sculpture, taxidermy, and fine art photography.

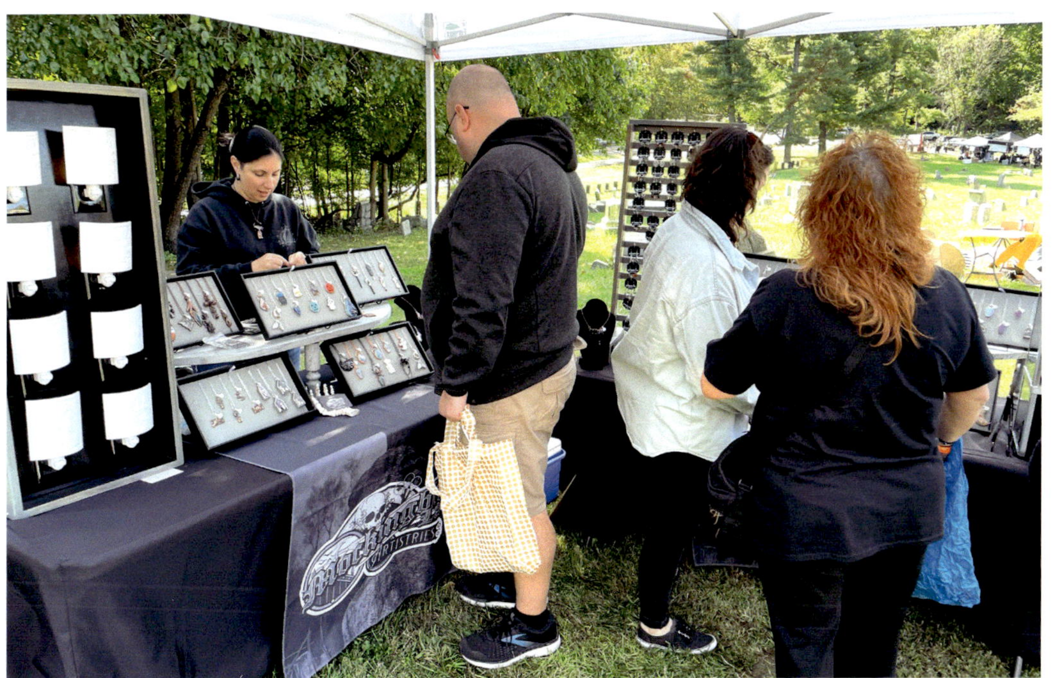

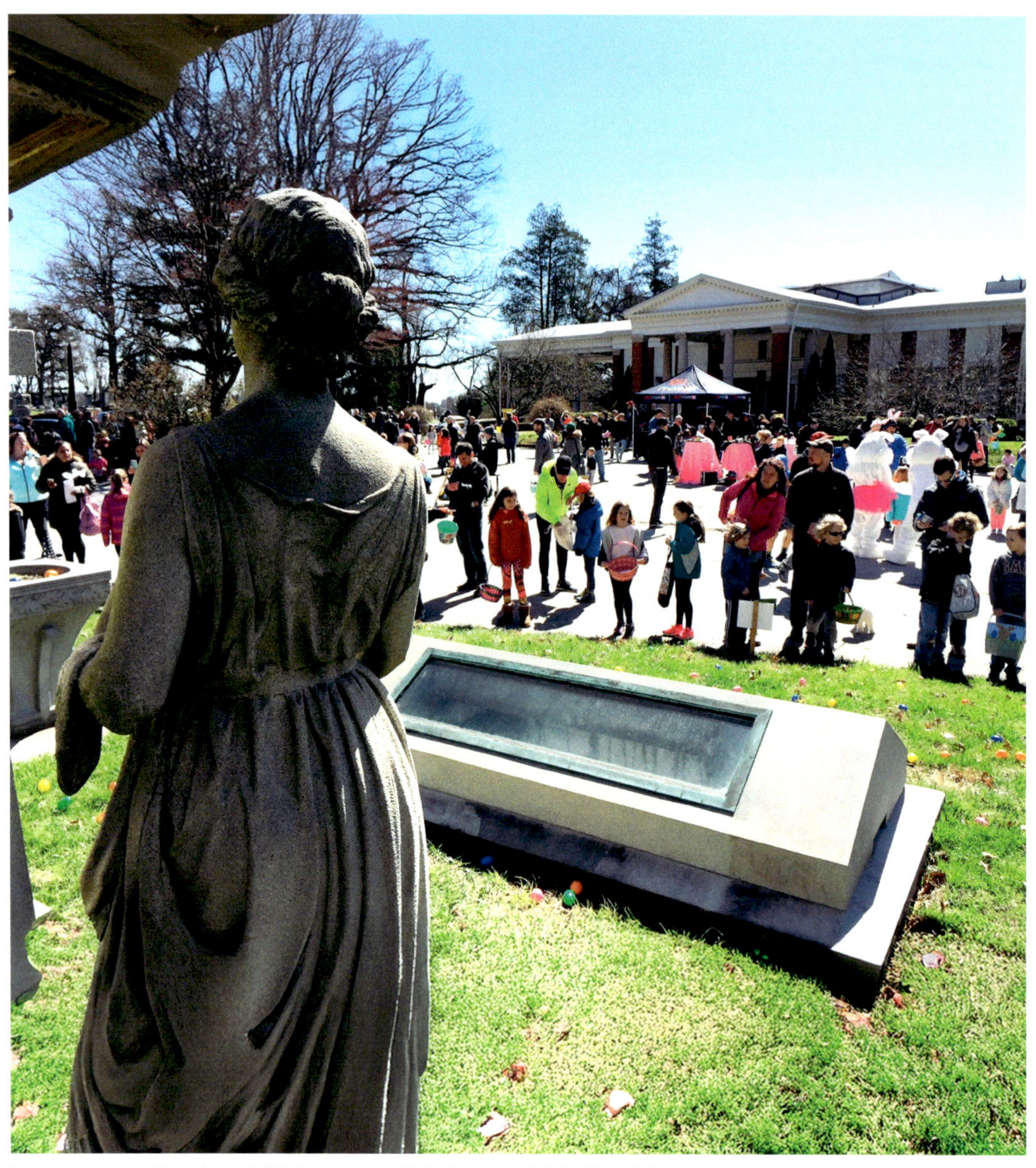

For many years, West Laurel Hill Cemetery in Bala Cynwyd, PA, held a children's Easter Egg Hunt, which was wildly popular.

8

MOUNT VERNON CEMETERY AND HAR HASETIM CEMETERY

Teetering on the Edge of Oblivion

Mount Vernon Cemetery, a 27-acre wilderness in the middle of Philadelphia, is mysterious, padlocked, and overgrown with trees and other foliage. Its immense Gothic arched entranceway is flanked by trumpeting marble angels that announce your entrance—if, in fact, you were allowed to enter. Most are not.

For decades, rumors were as rampant as the vines that pulled angels off their pedestals, as to why this 1856 Victorian sculpture garden was in such deplorable condition. Plot holders had to pay $25 to visit any of its 33,000 graves. Even descendants of the Drews and Barrymores had to pay for the groundskeeper to hack his way to the grave.

As with any abandoned cemetery, there is always a reason. In general terms, this property was willed by the owner to a relative who did not want it. Minimal upkeep was done to avoid public complaints. The fact that Mount Vernon has been neglected and kept under lock and key for over twenty years has kept it in an unusual state of preservation. Although the trees, vines, weeds, and ivy turned it into an arboreal prison, the iron border fencing has kept it safe from vandals—but not, unfortunately, from thieves or nature. Bronze mausoleum doors and stained-glass windows have disappeared. Nature's elements wore the roof off the gatehouse office and threatened to destroy the burial records.

After decades of neglect, preservationists took the cemetery's absentee landlord owner to court using a Pennsylvania law that enables conservators to save abandoned and blighted properties. The owner lost control of the property in 2021.[1]

The Philadelphia Community Development Coalition, which now has temporary ownership and control, is the conservator of the cemetery and has worked diligently with a volunteer Friends group to stabilize the historic cemetery. As of 2024, there is only access to the property if you visit during one of the Friends' official cleanup or tour days.

The Mount Vernon Cemetery Conservation Company (MVCCC) was formed with the goal of eventually taking ownership. In July 2024, the 26-acre cemetery was listed for sale for $1 million as part of a larger effort to preserve the space.[2, 3] The property had to be listed on the market before the MVCCC could become its default buyer. Mount Vernon's future is tenuous.

Another Philadelphia mystery is the abandoned Jewish cemetery in the woods of Gladwyne, a suburb of Philadelphia. Unlike Mount Vernon, you cannot see it. There is no public roadway passing by the property. For decades, no one knew where it was. Over time, many small private family burial grounds find themselves surrounded by private property. Har Hasetim, however, is not small. At nearly 1,000 burials, originally on 20 acres, this is a sizeable cemetery hidden from the road, surrounded by private homes and woods. You cannot visit, let alone see it, without permission from the new owners, nearby Beth David Reform Congregation.

Acquired by Beth David in 1997, the old cemetery had languished since its final burial in 1945. Since it was established in 1890, it faced financial hardship and real estate land grabs for decades, but somehow remained somewhat intact. Burial records were stored by an affiliated cemetery and are readily accessible. Abandoned and crumpling, taken over by nature, land-locked Har Hasetim continued to exist in its secretive location. Urban explorers would stumble upon it from time to time.

In 2011, Beth David set up a non-profit corporation to manage and restore Har Hasetim into a memorial park.[4] The Friends of Gladwyne Jewish Memorial Cemetery was formed to preserve 125 years of Jewish history and honor the people buried there, first-generation European immigrants who came to America in the late 1800s to escape persecution. The burial ground has been renamed "Gladwyne Jewish Memorial Cemetery." As you look at the before and after photos, you can appreciate the stunning and meticulous work that has been done to stabilize and restore the property. Quite breathtaking is the reconstruction and preservation of hundreds of broken grave markers, monuments, and cradle graves throughout the cemetery.

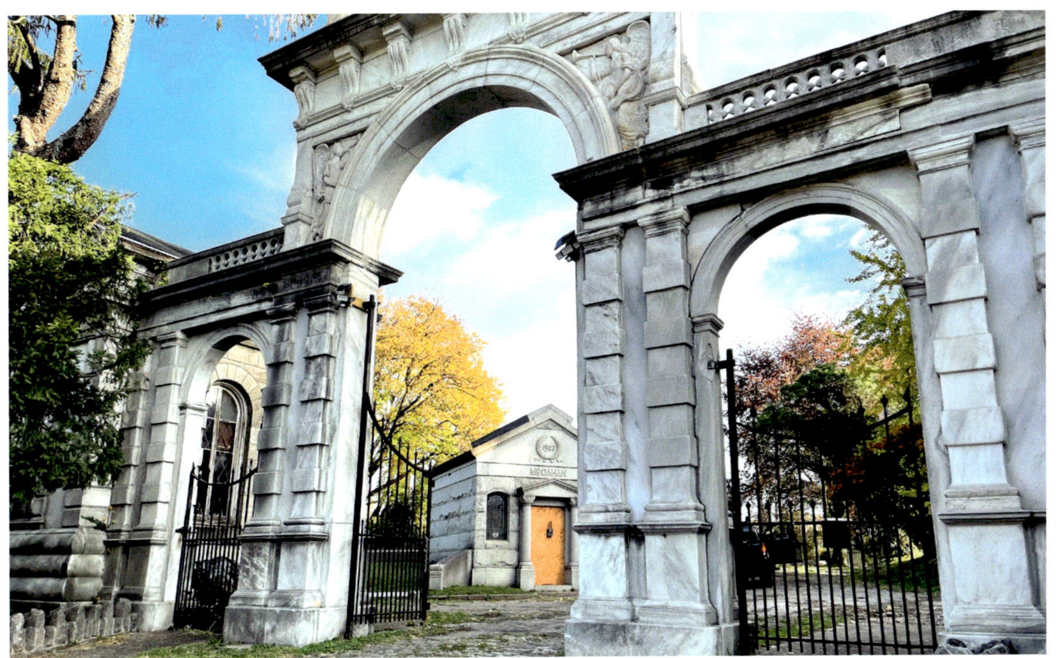

The stately marble arched entrance to Philadelphia's Mount Vernon Cemetery was designed by John Notman and built in 1858 at 3301 West Lehigh Avenue.

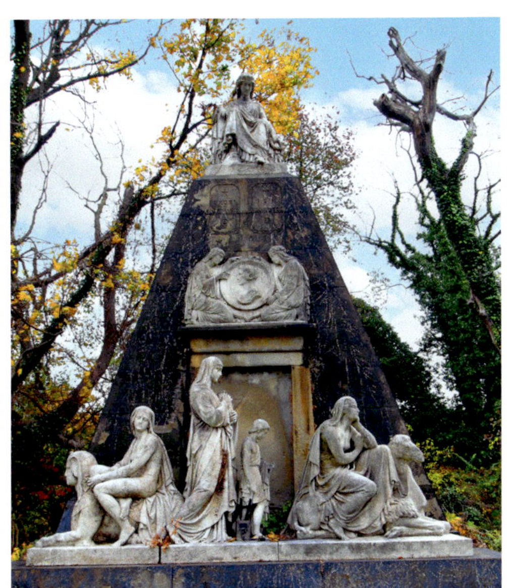

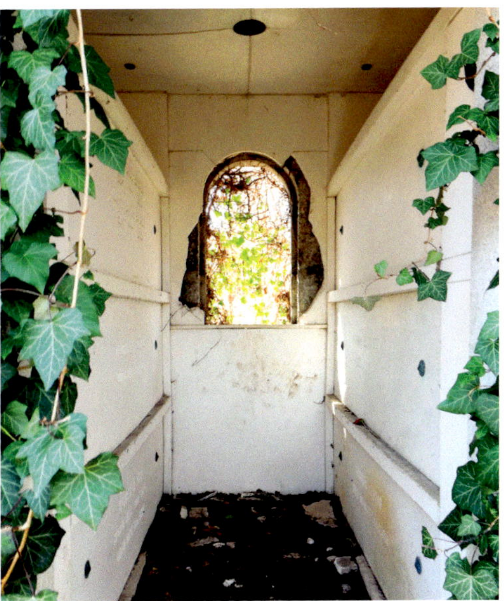

Above left: In winter when everything dies, glimpses can be had through the fence of marble monuments, headstones, and mausoleums. The Gardel Monument with its many allegorical figures in mourning is a memorial to Julia Hawks Gardel, a Philadelphia author and schoolteacher who died in 1859.

Above right: There is a black market for art objects like antique stained-glass windows (especially Tiffany) and a scrap market for bronze. The window has been torn from this mausoleum and the bronze doors are gone.

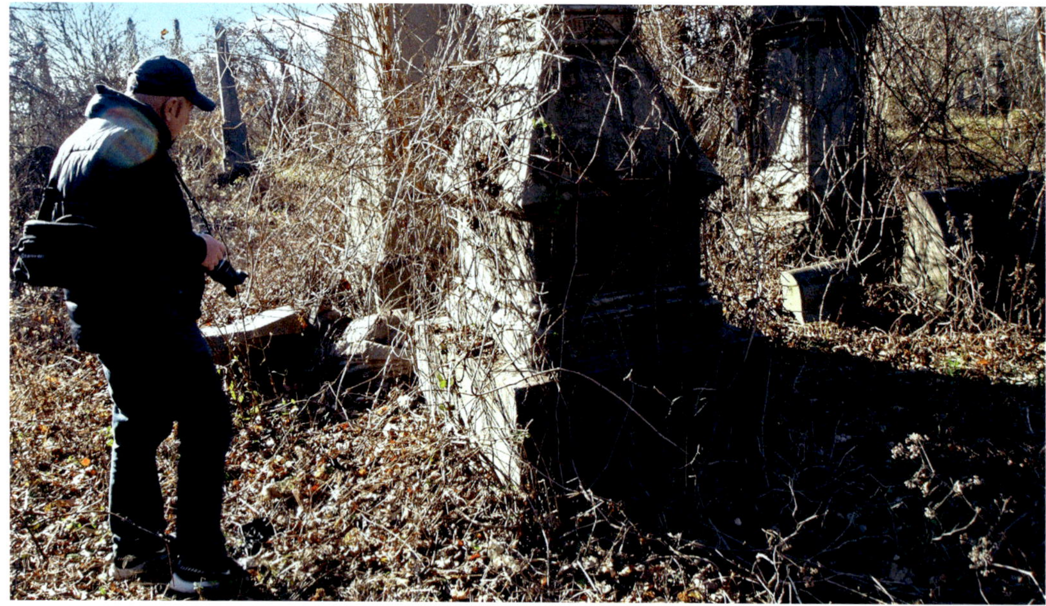

A Victorian-era sculpture garden suspended in time holds the interest of historians, artists, and preservationists, not to mention thrill-seekers. Wild animals, sunken graves, fallen monuments, uneven terrain, poison ivy, deer ticks—Mount Vernon has them all, hence the popularity of the documentation provided by the tenacious urban explorer.

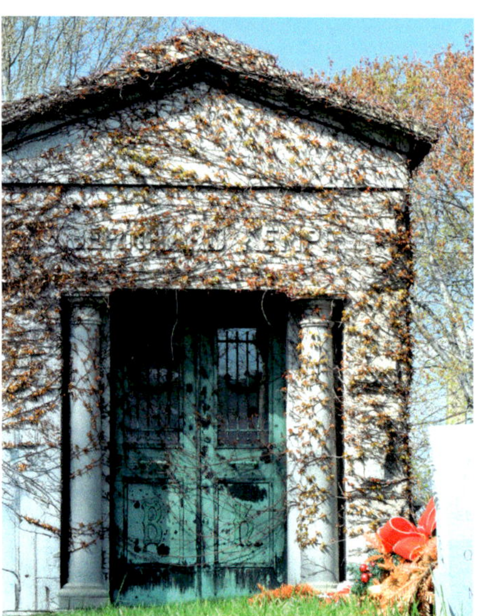

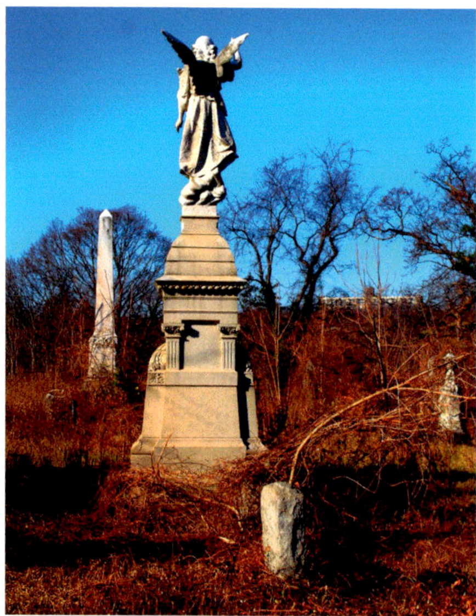

Above left: The theft of bronze mausoleum doors from many cemeteries occurs during economic downturns and when the price of scrap metal soars. At 2024 salvage prices ($2.00 per pound), a pair of 500-pound bronze doors would fetch $2,000 from a scrap metal dealer.

Above right: After decades of neglect, preservationists took the cemetery's absentee landlord owner to court using a Pennsylvania law that enables conservators to save abandoned and blighted properties. Burial records were moved when the roof of the vacated office building collapsed around 2012; as of 2024, the records have not been fully recovered.

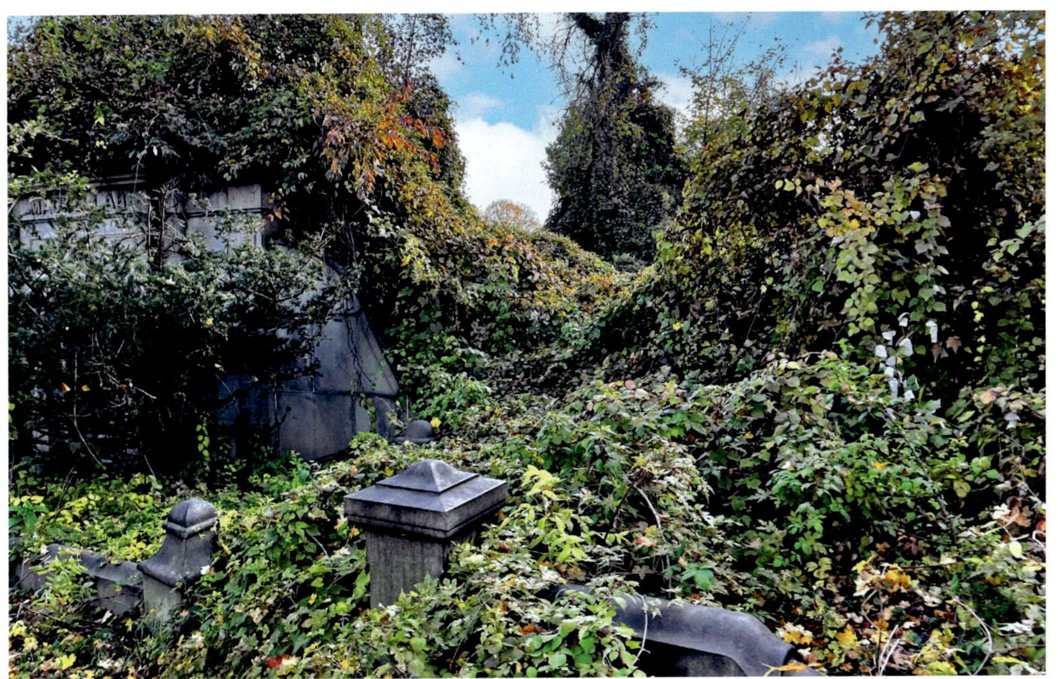

This "before" photo shows an overgrown section of Mount Vernon Cemetery on November 13, 2021, where the family plots of the Drew and Barrymore theatrical families are buried.

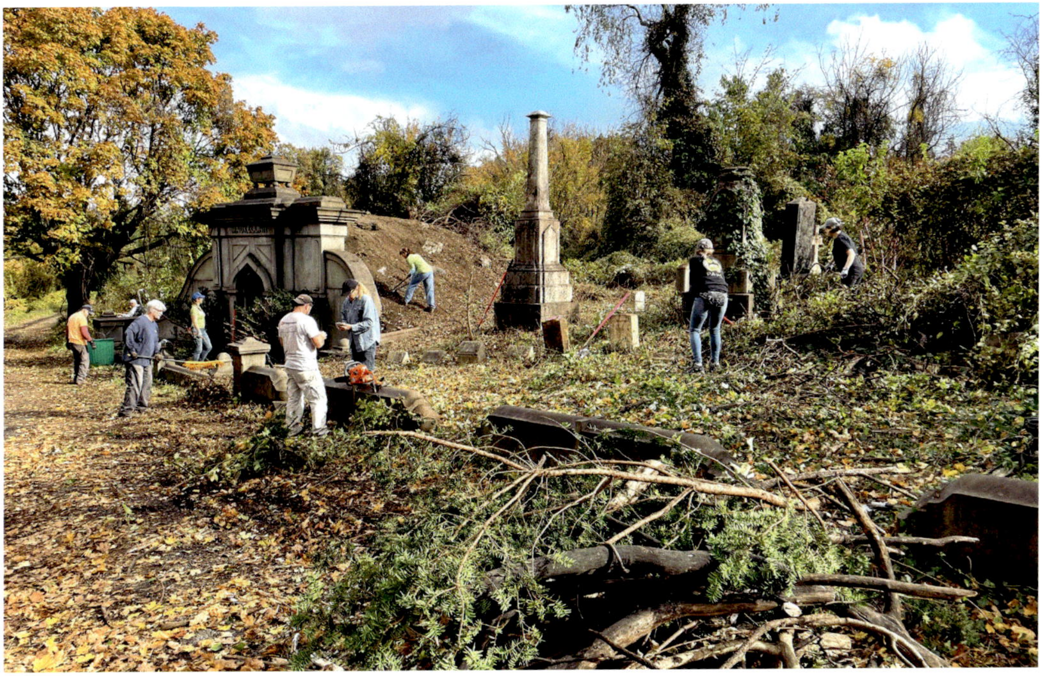

This "after" photo on November 13, 2021, shows the result after volunteers from the Friends of Mount Moriah Cemetery, Inc. cleared the grounds near the plots of the Drew and Barrymore families.

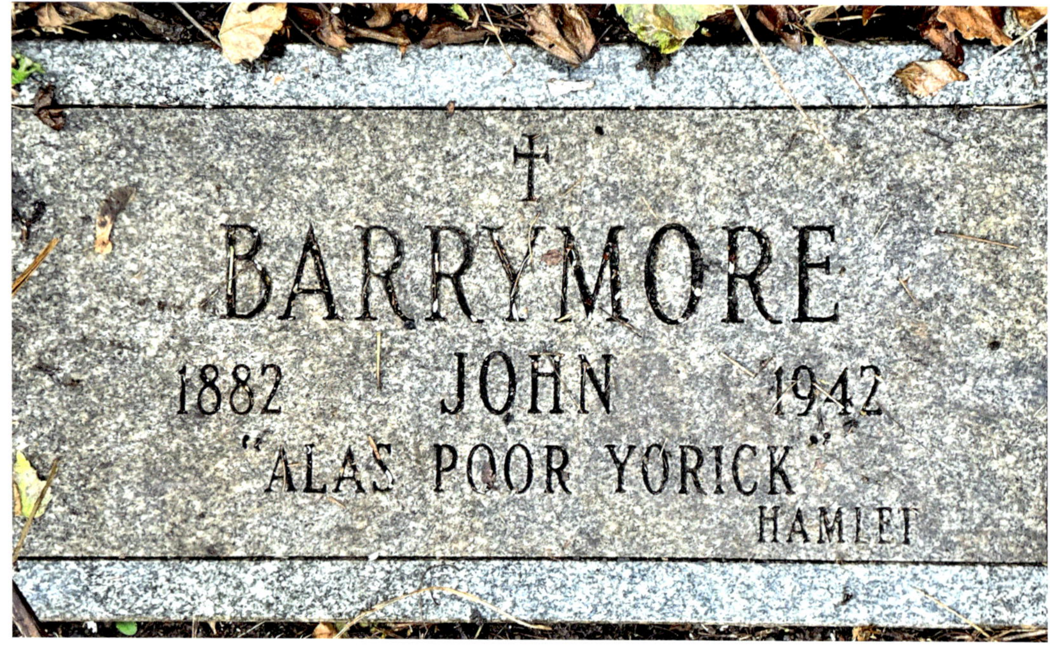

The grave marker of John Barrymore (actress Drew Barrymore's grandfather) is shown in Mount Vernon Cemetery. He was originally entombed in a mausoleum at Calvary Cemetery in Los Angeles. In 1980, his son, John Drew Barrymore, had the casket removed, the body cremated, and the ashes interred in the Drew-Barrymore plot in Mount Vernon.

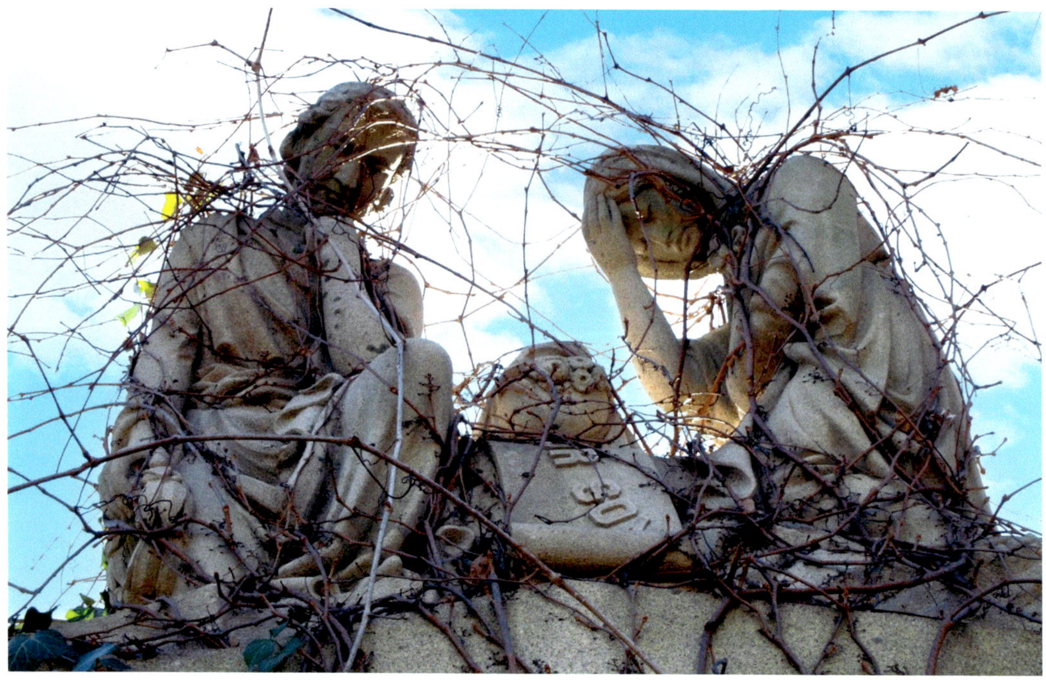

Unique statuary is abundant in the 26-acre Victorian sculpture garden that is Mount Vernon Cemetery (est. 1856). To visit, please check the Facebook site, "Family and Friends of Mount Vernon Cemetery."

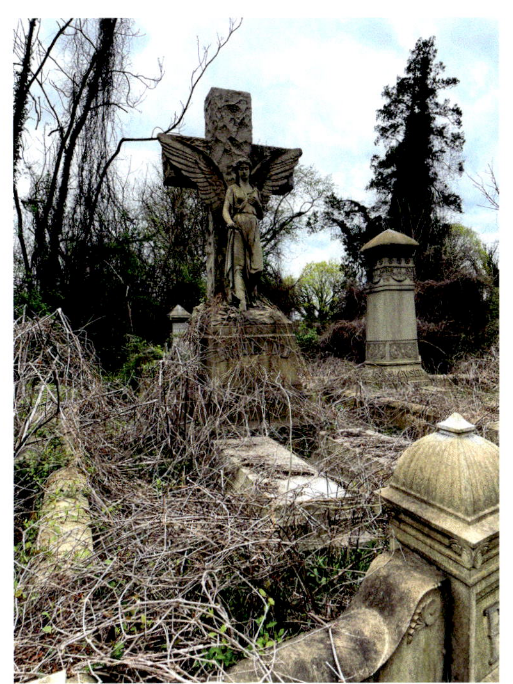

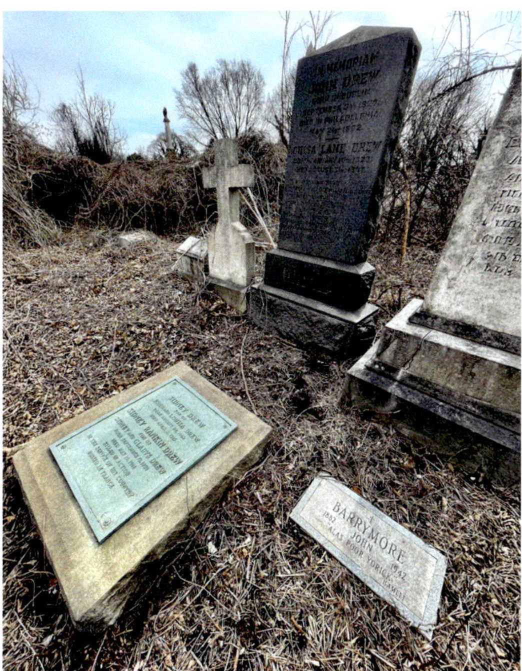

Above left: Magnificent family plots at Mount Vernon Cemetery have stood the test of time, but not of nature. Falling trees knock monuments over, creeping vines pull angels off their pedestals.

Above right: The Drew and Barrymore family plot at Mount Vernon Cemetery, Philadelphia, is an historical chapter in professional theater. If not tended to, the entire plot becomes covered with weeds, thorns, and mile-a-minute invasive vines in a few months' time.

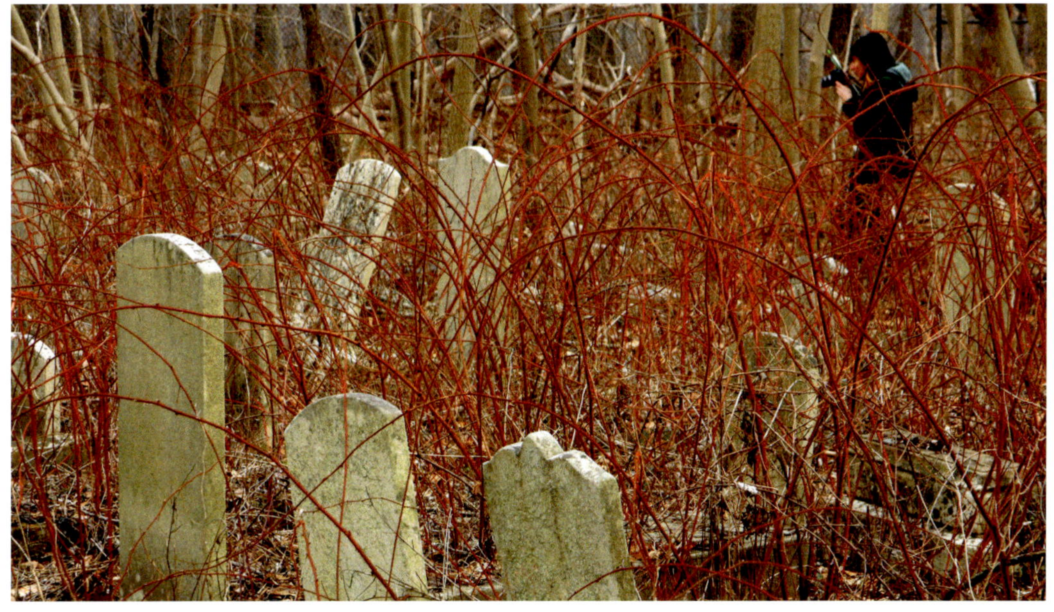

Acres of prickly wineberry vines had spread across the majority of the graves at Har Hasetim Cemetery in Gladwyne, PA. Years of work by volunteers, sponsored by Friends of the Gladwyne Jewish Memorial Cemetery, have eradicated the invasive plants.

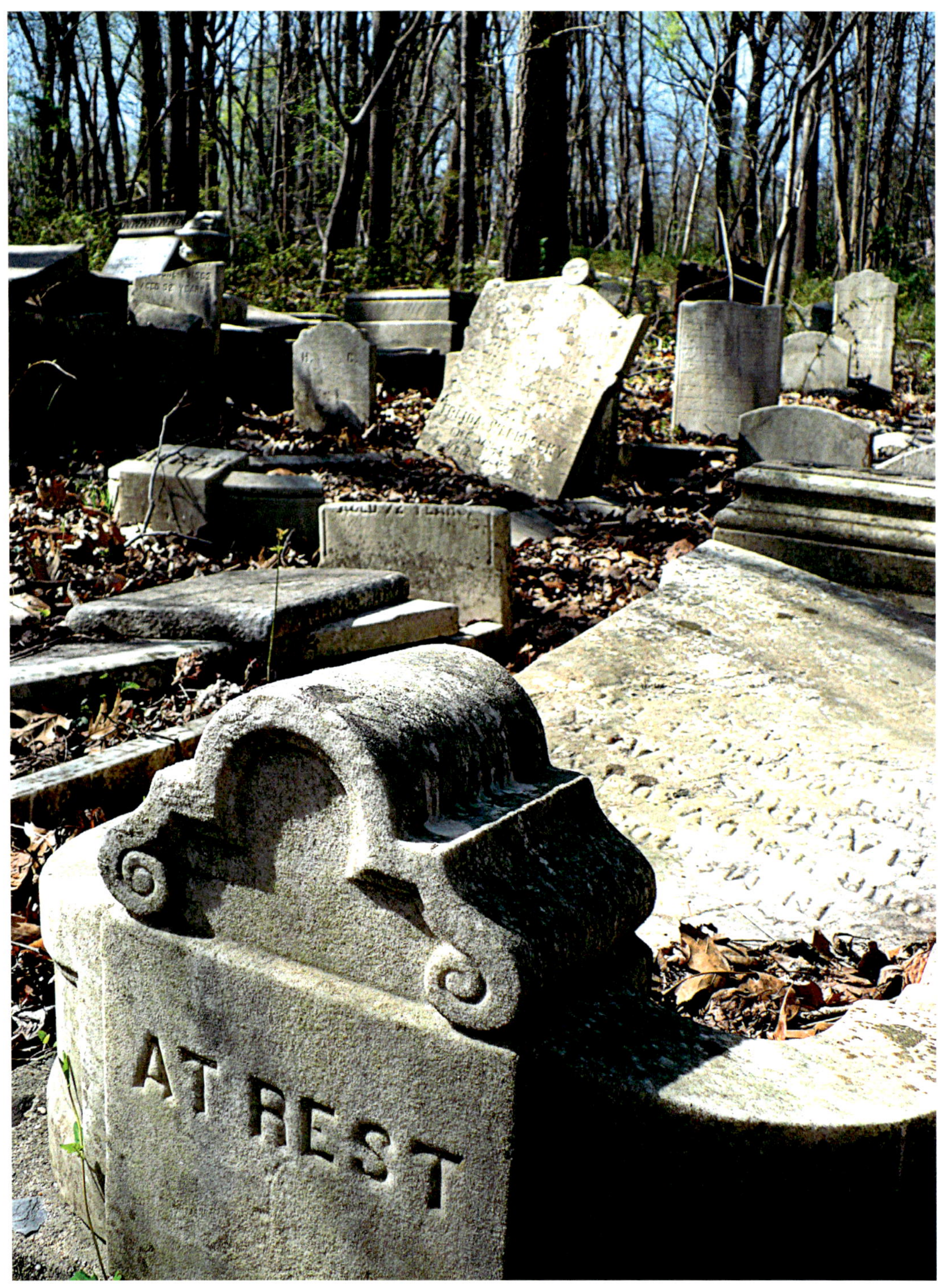

Mostly marble grave markers and cradle graves adorn the terraced landscape of Har Hasetim. The stones shown in this photo are currently being reassembled and restored by professionals. Safety is always an issue in any cemetery, as heavy stones can topple and cause injury.

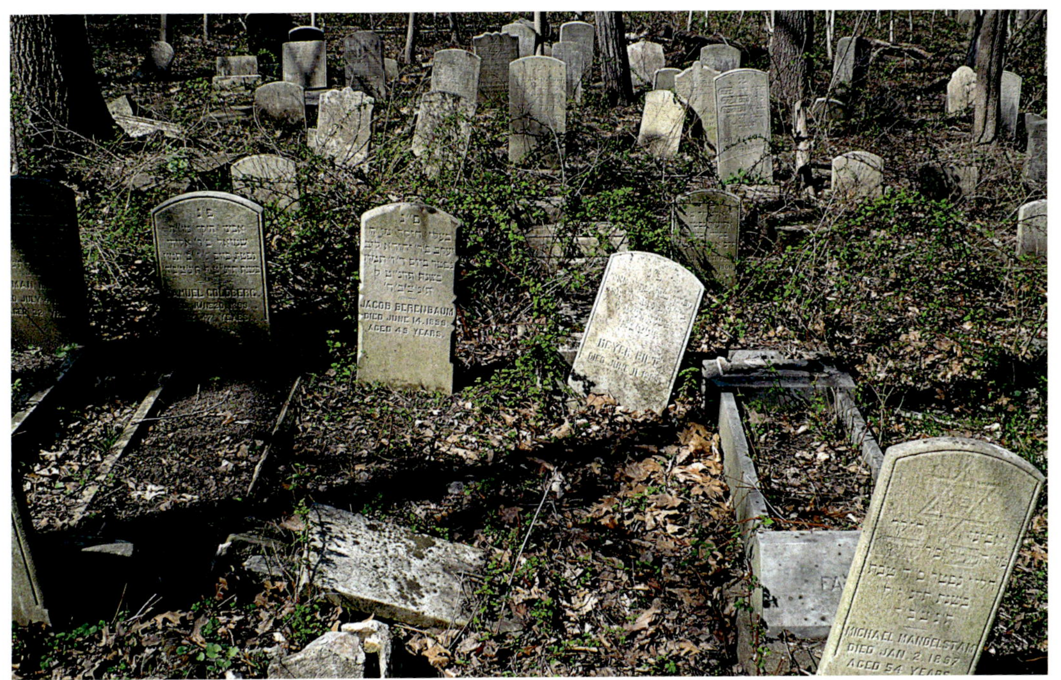

Har Hasetim is surrounded by woods, in addition to stately homes with private tennis courts. Some of the trees that grew since the cemetery was abandoned in 1945 had fallen and caused damage to the stones.

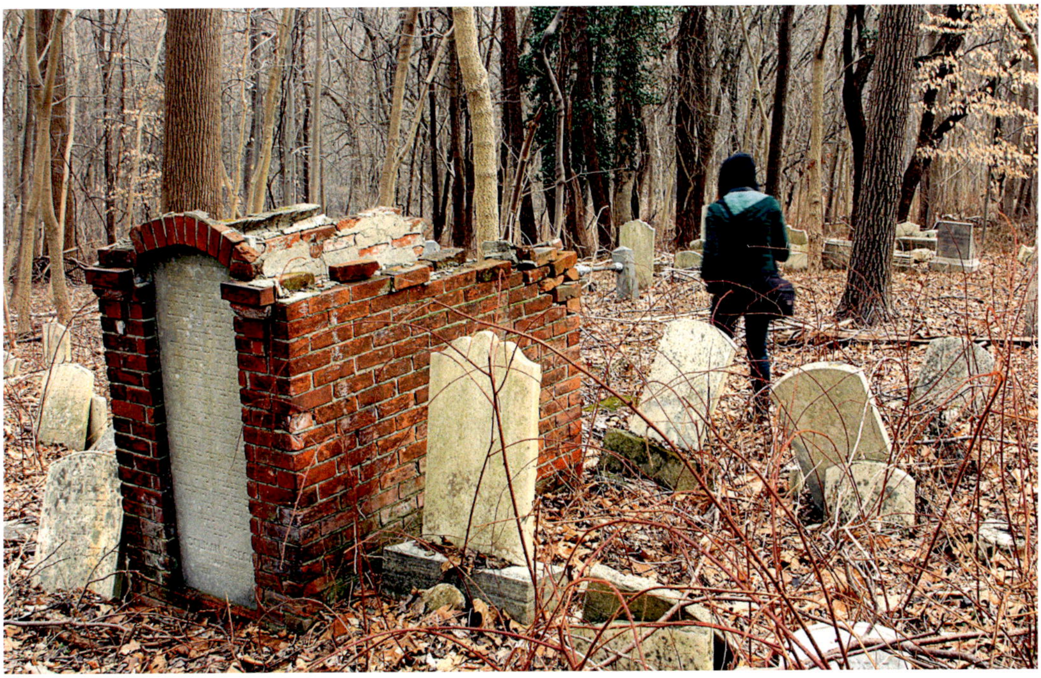

Prior to Beth David beginning restoration work at Har Hasetim Cemetery, the location of, and access to the cemetery was unclear. If you drive up the only access road leading to the cemetery, you would likely be asked to leave by any one of several homeowners whose homes surround the property—you are in their driveway.

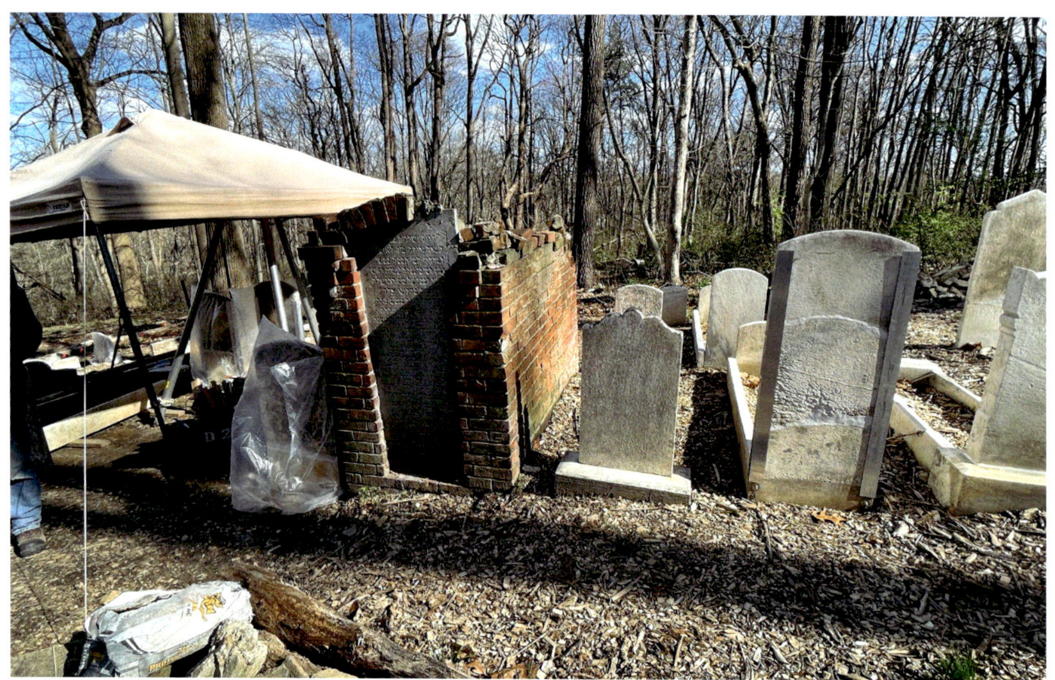

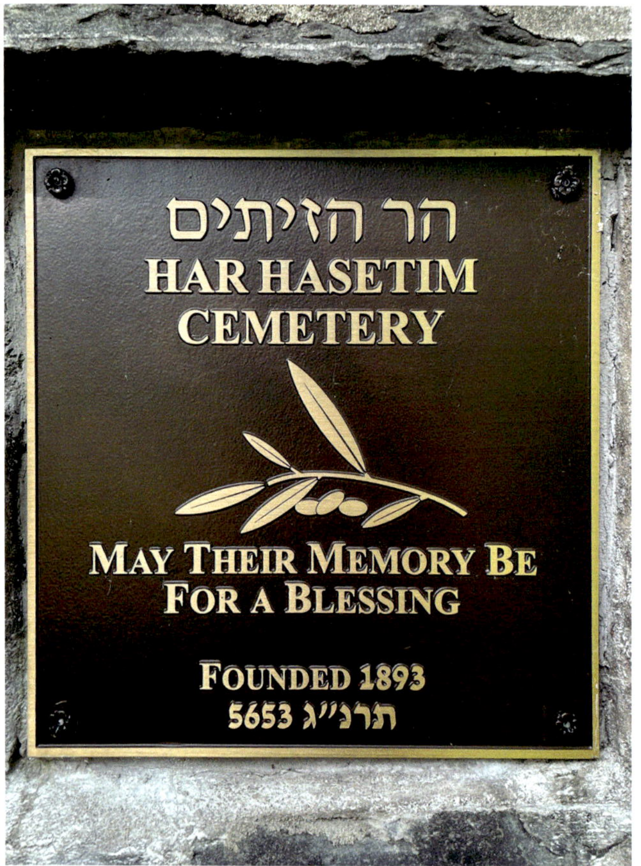

Above: Restoration work on the grave markers, monuments, and other structures within Har Hasetim continues. To visit, donate, or volunteer, please contact the Friends group on their website: www.gladwynejewishcemetery.org.

Left: Har Hasetim has been renamed "Gladwyne Jewish Memorial Cemetery" by the volunteer Friends group, sponsored by nearby Beth David Reform Congregation. The stone entrance pillars have been reconstructed, with a gate and plaque installed.

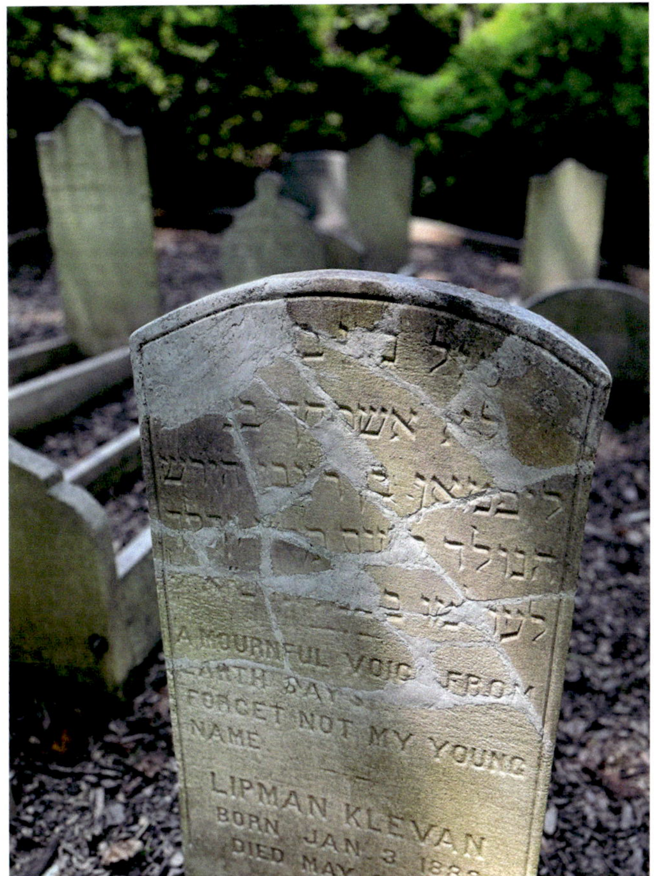

Right: "Forget not my young name," a heartfelt inscription on a broken grave marker that was reassembled in Har Hasetim. With death on the doorstep, many consider their own mortality, along with the possibility of being forgotten. Consider the words, "keep me in your heart for a while," from a song written by Warren Zevon as he was dying of cancer in 2008.

Below: The cemetery, Har Hasetim, was named after the Jewish Cemetery on the Mount of Olives, the oldest and most important Jewish cemetery in Jerusalem. Since 2012, many volunteers have performed the solemn and rewarding work of tending these graves.

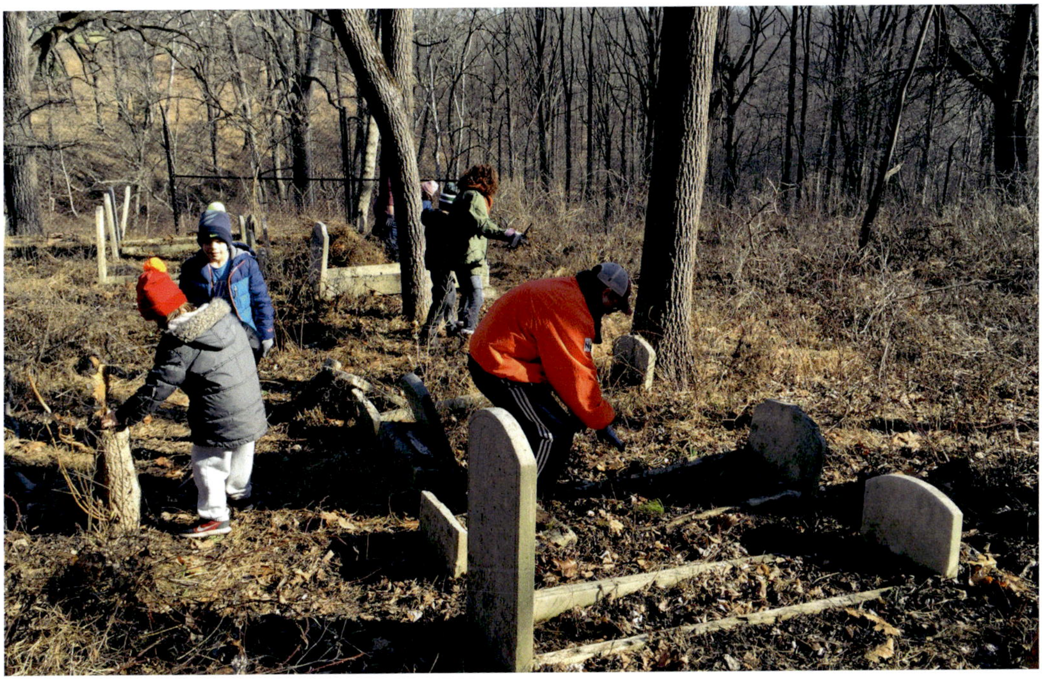

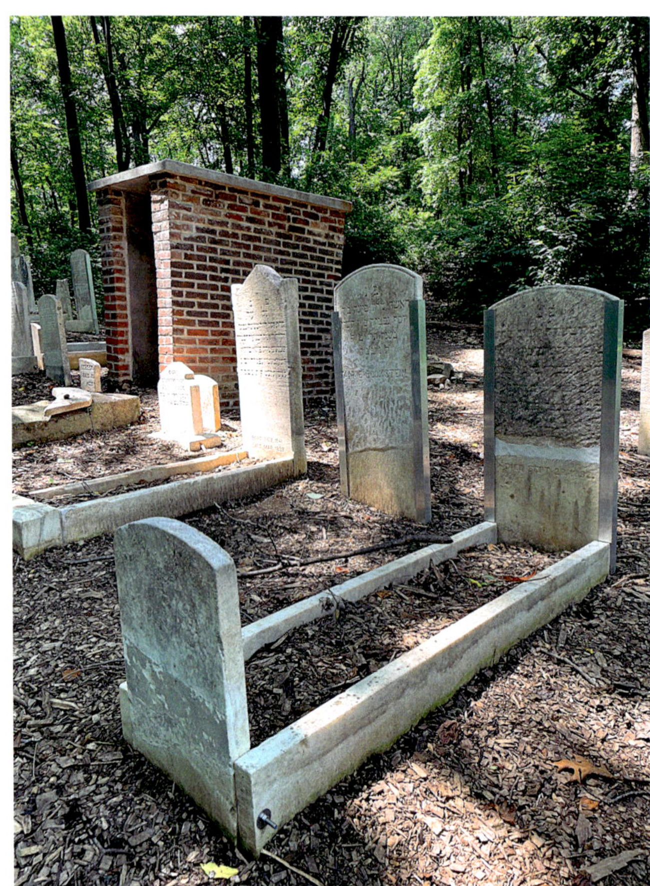

Left: This reconstructed brick crypt and surrounding cradle graves are being painstakingly restored by local masons and conservators from the company Grave Stone Matters. Visitors continually witness improvements to the cemetery as more and more graves are repaired, cleaned, and preserved for future generations.

Below: Cleaned and reconstructed cradle gravestones have made grave identification and transcription possible at Har Hasetim. Genealogic research is conducted by the Friends for descendants of those buried in the cemetery.

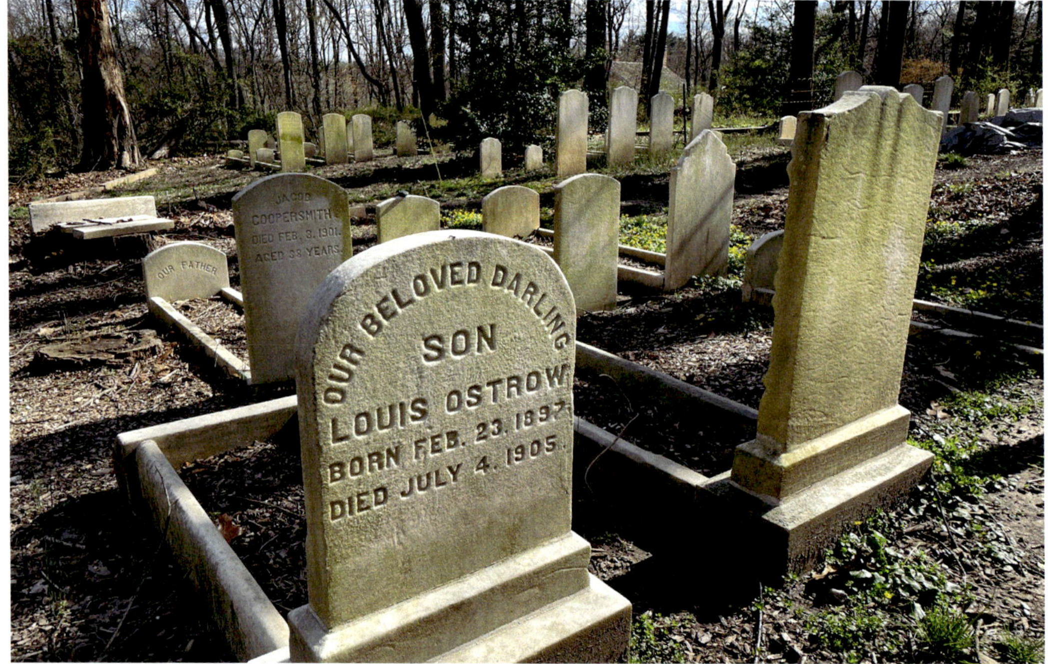

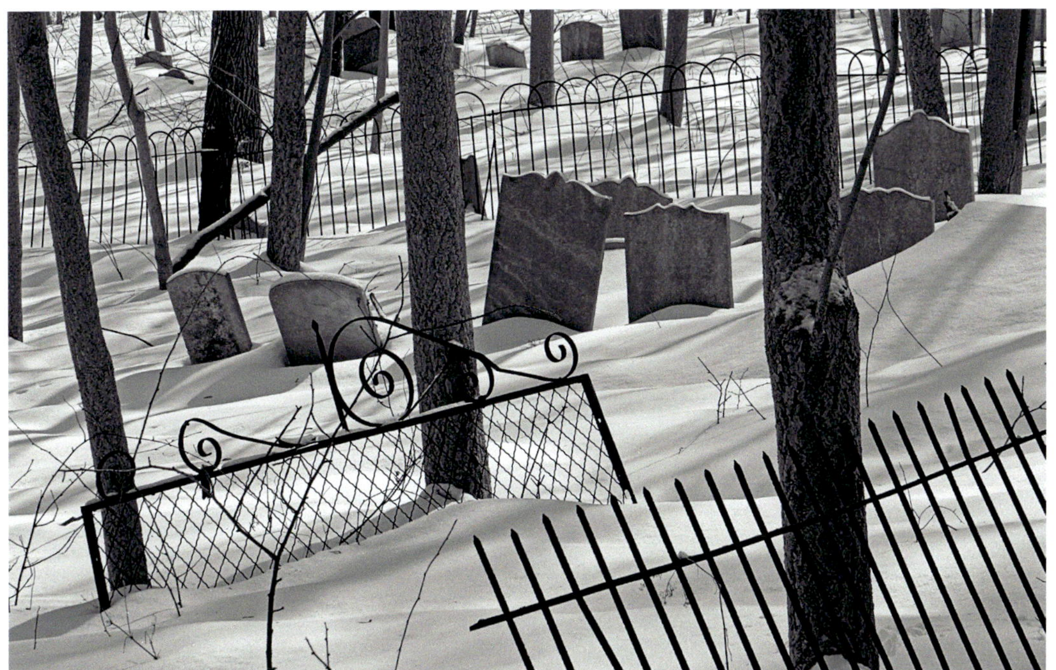

Above: Research by the Friends group indicates that many benevolent organizations purchased plots in Har Hasetim for their members. Remnants of fencing still exists to delineate these areas.

Right: Since 2012, invasive trees have been cleared from around graves, then chipped and spread for ground coverage. Felled trees have been repurposed to create plot borders and to line the walking paths that meander through Har Hasetim.

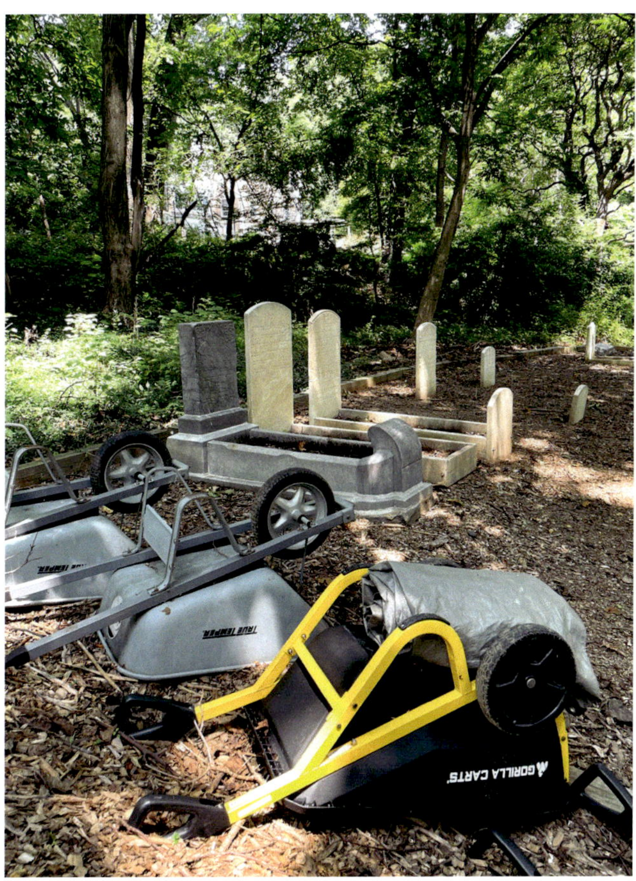

CONCLUSION

VOLUNTEERISM AND RESPECT FOR THE PAST

Perhaps the most important point to be made regarding Philadelphia's abandoned and derelict cemeteries was made by Alexandra Mosca.[1] She states that whatever the size of a cemetery, it tells part of the story of a city's history. If a cemetery is missing, so is that chapter from the city's past. Sometimes, we don't even know a cemetery is in trouble. Consider the situation that Wenonah Cemetery found itself in 2013.

Wenonah is a small community in south Jersey, across the Delaware River from Philadelphia. Bill's family lives there. In 2006, Bill's nine-year-old son died and was laid to rest in the cemetery. Family members would visit regularly, but in 2012, they were dismayed to see the grounds not being maintained. Inquiries led to the fact that the owner could no longer care for the property. Bill and other neighbors volunteered to cut the grass.

In 2014, the Wenonah Cemetery Association was formed as receiver of the cemetery. The non-profit is led by a board of directors (Bill and two other volunteers). In 2019, Bill retired from his career and has been the full-time volunteer face of this active cemetery—planning burials, maintaining the grounds, expanding services, organizing events, and fundraising for improvements like new roads, signage, and a columbarium. Few people realize what happened, or what could have happened to Wenonah Cemetery if it had not been for Bill and a handful of other volunteers. Similar plights have befallen many cemeteries, large and small. Keeping cemeteries alive is vital. By respecting the past, we show respect for ourselves.

The past, sometimes, has a way of reminding us of its continued presence. When we least expect it, bones appear when Philadelphians dig. In 2001, the water company inadvertently dug into some burials on Washington Avenue in south Philadelphia.

The unmarked Bishops' Burial Ground was in the way of a new water main, and the backhoe sliced through a cross-section of full-coffin burials. Digging temporarily ceased, archeologists from Temple University called in, and seventeen bodies removed to Laurel Hill Cemetery. No legal protocol exists for such projects, but the water line work needed to continue. It was decided to remove only the bodies necessary for the pipes to be laid, and work around the remaining bodies without disturbing them.

The first documented occurrence of such an event in Philadelphia was in 1769, so discovering an unknown graveyard is not a recent development. As the Philadelphia Archaeological Forum (PAF) has stated, the legal and ethical issues surrounding land development in an area of old burials requires more specificity with clear guidelines, rules, and regulations.[2]

To advise developers in managing burial remains more respectfully, PAF published an extensive geographical map and database in 2018 that includes more than 200 unmarked historic burial places in Philadelphia.[3] As advocates for those interred in abandoned and forgotten cemeteries in the city, PAF is actively communicating the need for clearer municipal laws that compel developers to handle burial remains respectfully. In 2024, there were tentative plans to build a new Philadelphia 76ers basketball arena in Center City, Philadelphia. This would have replaced the shopping mall between Tenth and Eleventh Streets, from Market Street to Chinatown. One would hope the developers consulted the PAF map and were aware of the two (currently underground and unmarked) cemeteries that would be disturbed. The 1822 Fifth Presbyterian Church graveyard at Tenth and Cuthbert Streets was closed in 1903 and the 1823 First African Baptist Church graveyard at Eleventh and Market Streets was closed in 1837.

Thousands of people volunteer their time and skills to stabilize, restore, and preserve old graveyards. Though their reasons vary, all volunteers have one common motivator—respect for the past. It is easy to point out examples of our callousness, but people can also exhibit empathy and care. For example, there is nothing left of the mine fire ghost town of Centralia, PA, except for two cemeteries. All the houses are gone, and the streets are overgrown with trees. However, churches from neighboring towns continue to maintain these cemeteries.

Many get an uneasy feeling about abandoned cemeteries, or when they see a headstone out of context, perhaps in an antique shop or used as a prop on a miniature golf course. Annette Stott suggests that this is because of the personality that stone has acquired.[4] The person whose grave it marked is gone, so the stone literally becomes a person substitute. When we see abandoned stones, abandoned cemeteries, perhaps we think of abandoned, forgotten people. This may cause us to consider our own mortality and the possibility of being forgotten ourselves. So let's maintain what we still have and respect what we've lost.

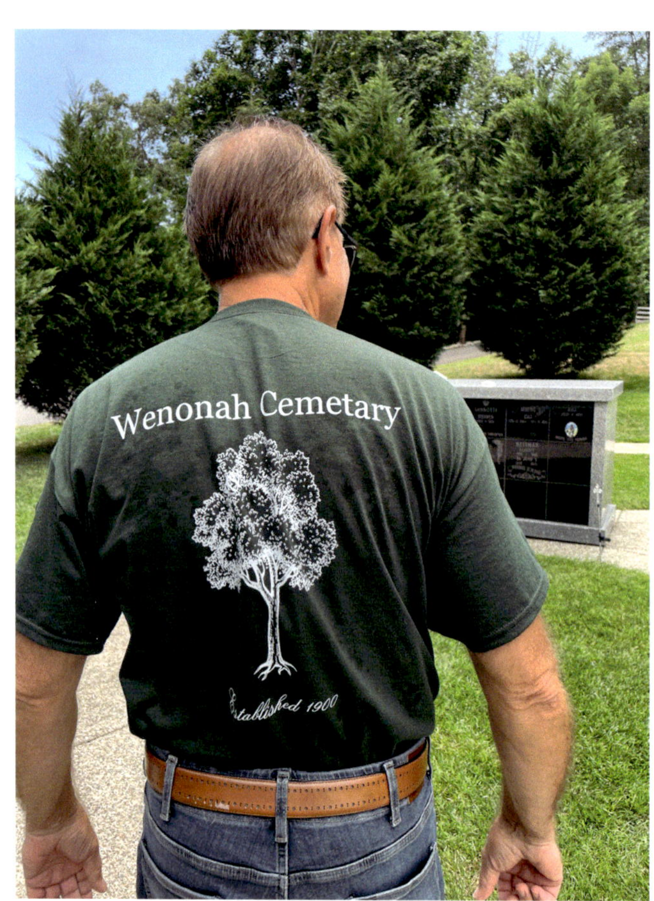

Left: Bill checks on the grounds of Wenonah Cemetery, where he volunteers as superintendent. The work allows him to be near his nine-year-old son who is buried in the cemetery.

Below: A grave marker was set at Laurel Hill Cemetery at the site where remains were reinterred from Bishop's Burial Ground in 2006. Only the remains of seventeen people were relocated from the water company dig at Eighth Street and Washington Avenue; all remaining bodies from this 1824 Burial Ground were left undisturbed.

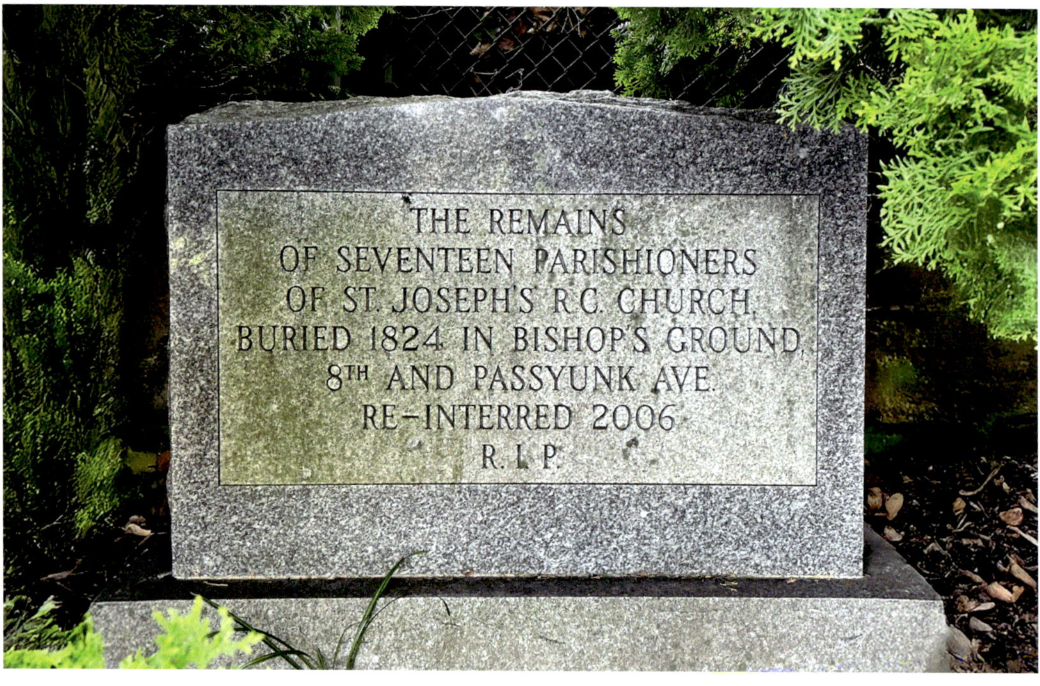

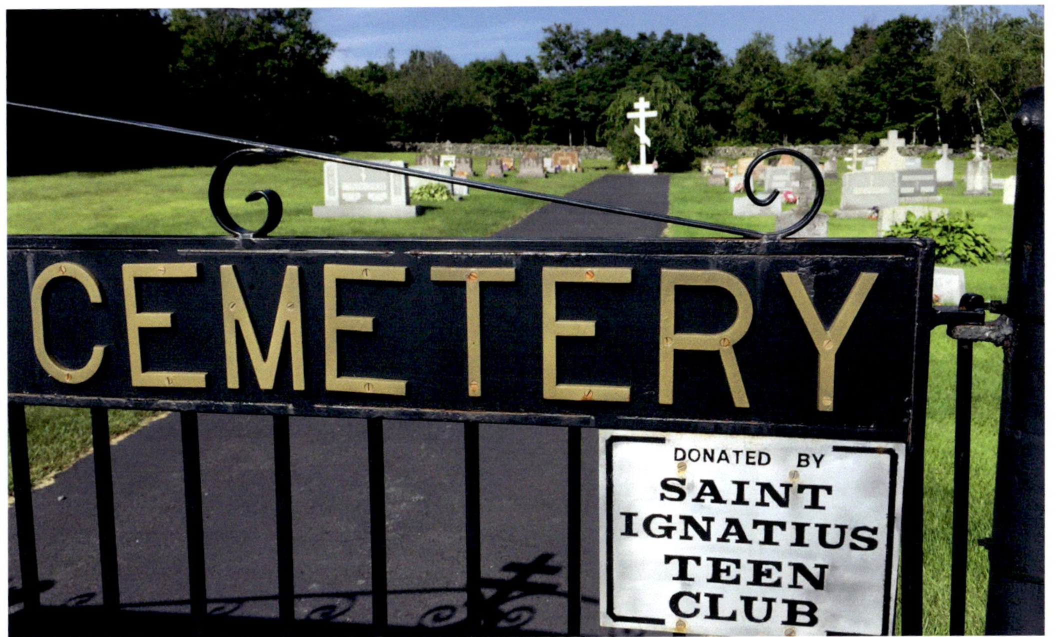

Saints Peter and Paul Cemetery is one of two cemeteries still in existence in the mine fire ghost town of Centralia, PA. It continues to be maintained by a church in a nearby town. The cemeteries, along with a few homes of residents who live off the grid are the only properties in Centralia that have not been destroyed.

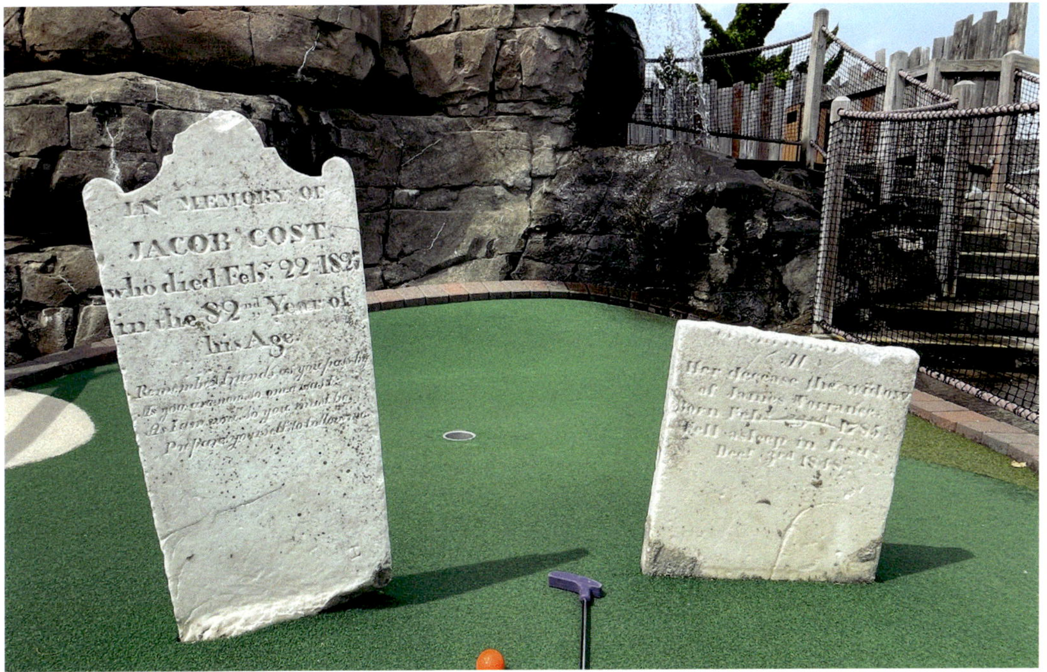

Headstones mark the hole on a miniature golf course at the Fantasy Island Amusement Park on Long Beach Island, New Jersey. According to www.findagrave.com, Cost is, or was buried in the Cost Family Cemetery in Jefferson, Frederick County, Maryland. How his stone ended up here is a mystery. It is typical, however, that small family cemeteries throughout America were removed over time as large farms and estates were sold off in parcels.

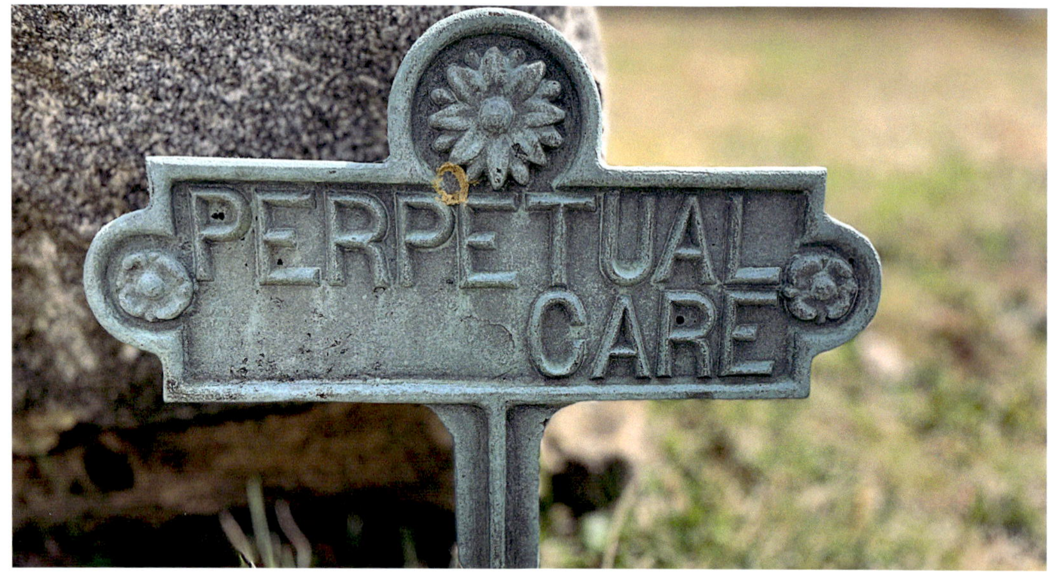

The irony of "perpetual care" is that hundreds of thousands of Philadelphia graves have been disturbed since the 1930s when that concept was initiated. People paid for perpetual care, yet the remains were dug up and moved. Generally, if property values are not high near the area of the cemetery where your loved ones are buried, their graves are probably safe. Otherwise, the city may evict them in the name of progress.

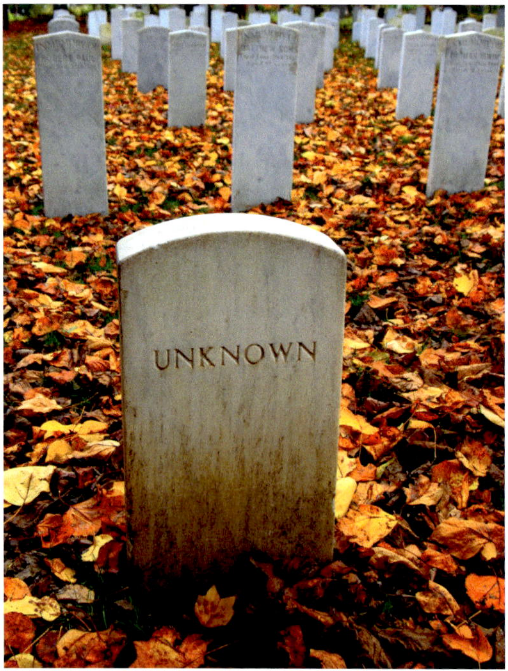

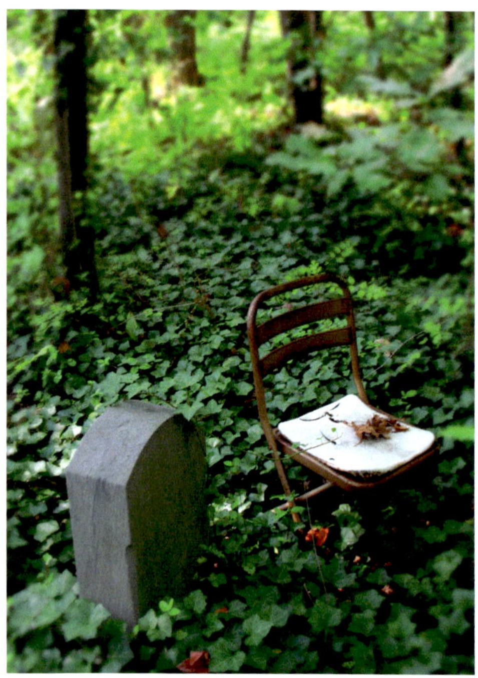

Above left: This unknown military veteran rests in the Naval Asylum plot at Philadelphia's Mount Moriah Cemetery. The plot is on the Yeadon, PA, side of the cemetery, in Delaware County. The original Naval Asylum, part of Biddle Hall on Gray's Ferry Avenue, was the nation's first retirement home established by the federal government for the care of disabled navy officers, seamen, and marines.

Above right: Lonely graves sit off in the woods of Mount Peace Cemetery, in Lawnside, New Jersey.

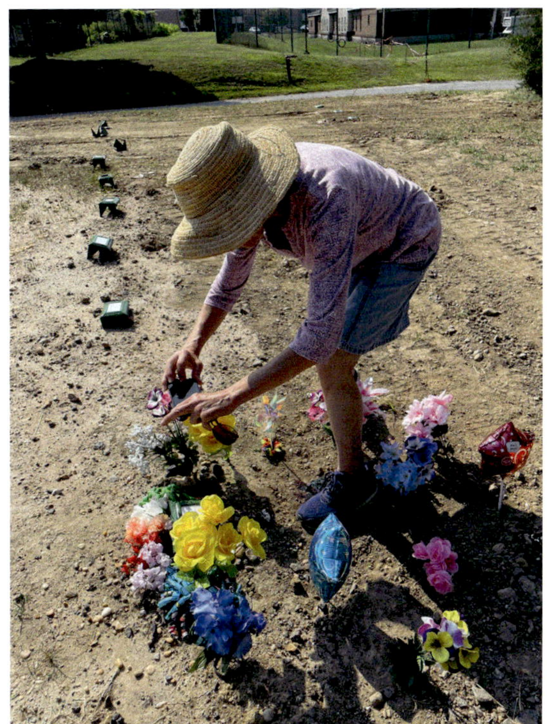

Faith Kuehn tends graves of former psychiatric patients in the Potters' Field of the Delaware State Hospital, New Castle, Delaware. "This is an opportunity to provide a measure of respect and dignity for people who probably struggled with that during their life … these graves here represent people who are part of the human family, just like you and me.'" (*whyy.org/articles/restoring-respect-and-dignity-to-777-souls-who-died-at-delaware-psychiatric-hospital-and-were-buried-in-numbered-graves*)

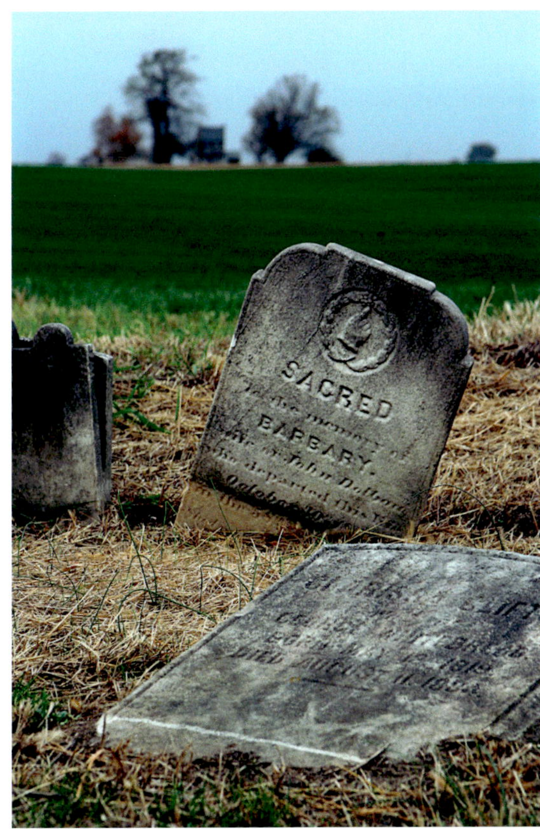

Grave markers such as those seen here on a farm in Salem County, New Jersey, are typical of family cemeteries. As farmland is divided up and sold in parcels over the years, the small burial grounds become islands between properties. Sometimes they are just built over and disappear.

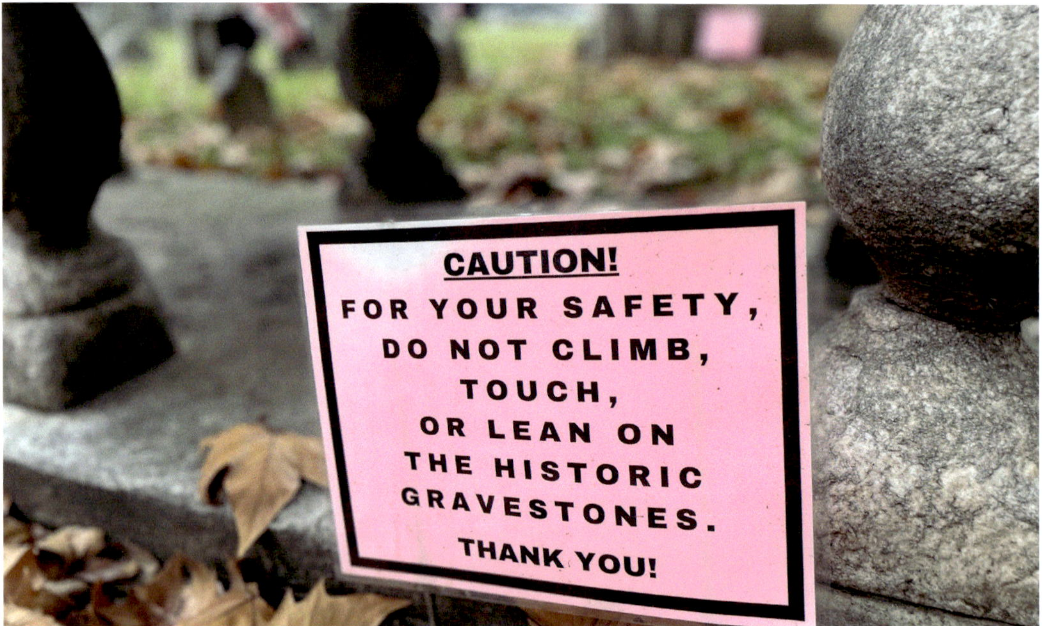

Signs are beginning to pop up in old graveyards (the burial ground of a church) and cemeteries warning people of the dangers of falling grave markers. People have been injured and killed by gravestones falling on them. They are not as solidly mounted as they might appear! This sign is in the graveyard of Old Pine Presbyterian Church (est. 1768) at Fourth and Pine Street, in Philadelphia.

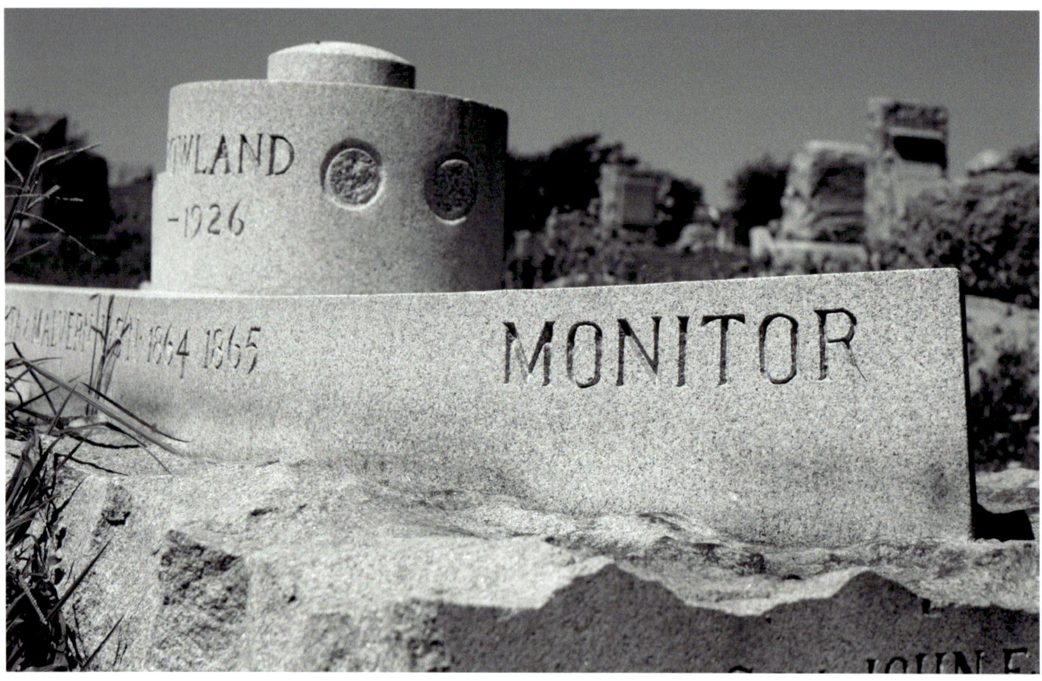

One of the many historic monuments in Philadelphia's Mount Moriah Cemetery is a granite-carved rendition of one of the Civil War ironclad warships, of Monitor and Merrimac fame. Unfortunately, the sculpture has suffered damage, likely caused by vandals.

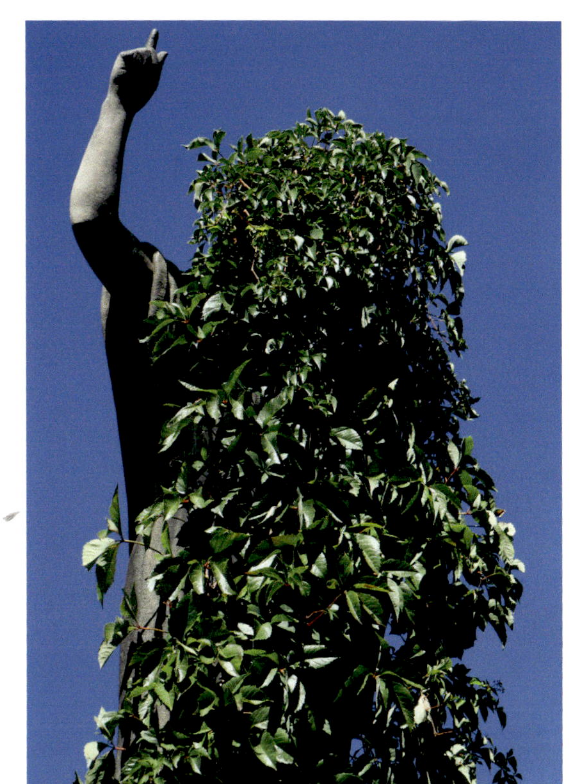

Landscaping challenges can be enormous in cemeteries with little funding. Not only can vines and other foliage conceal the beauty of the sculptures, but over time, they can pull the statues off their pedestals.

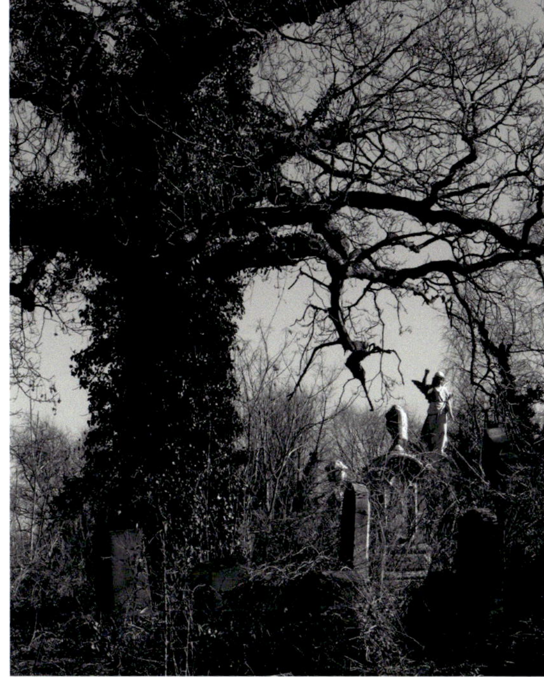

The beauty of an abandoned angel in Philadelphia's Mount Vernon Cemetery is hidden from the appreciative eye of the public. As 2006 executive director of Laurel Hill Cemetery, Ross Mitchell, said, "Realize that not all cemeteries are very depressing places.... If you look at the monuments and the sculpture in Laurel Hill you know these people wanted these monuments to be seen." (*www.stoneangels.net/ross-mitchell-part-8-visiting-laurel-hill-why-the-cemetery-is-a-celebration-of-life*)

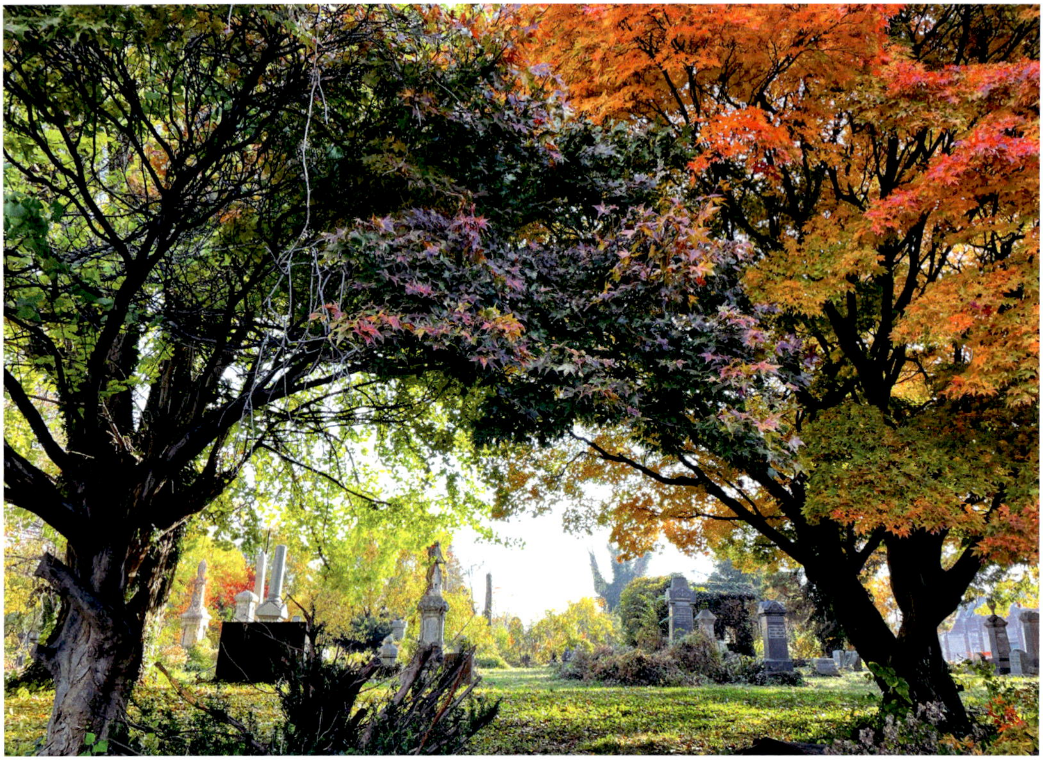

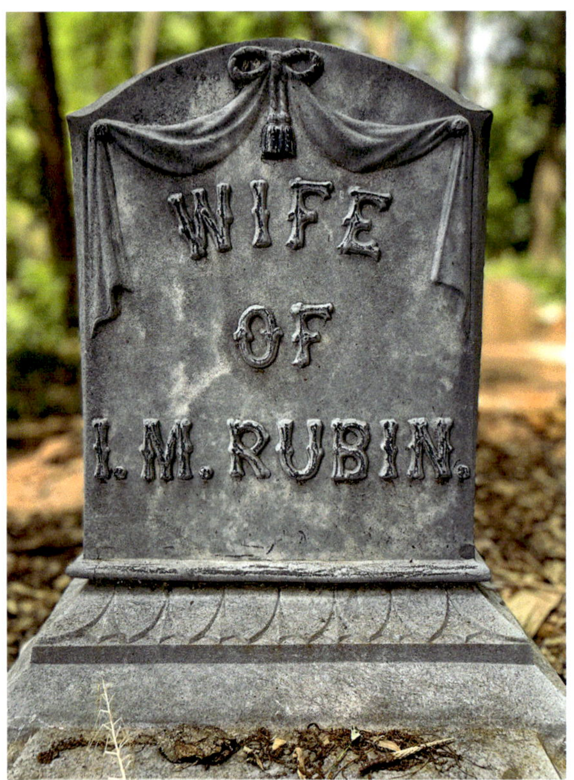

Above: One way to show respect for the past is to embrace it, and care for it. Philadelphia's Mount Vernon Cemetery is shown after volunteers had cleared an area and mowed the grass. The goal is for the Mount Vernon Cemetery Conservation Company, a nonprofit, to take over and make it into an active cemetery and public green space for the neighborhood.

Left: We draw the curtain on this book, much as our ancestors symbolically drew the curtain on life. This rare and unusual zinc (or "white bronze") grave marker in the formerly abandoned Gladwyne Jewish Memorial Cemetery is from a line of monuments made by the Monumental Bronze Company (1873–1914) of Bridgeport, Connecticut. It is being cared for by conscientious volunteers, along with acres of marble grave markers.

ENDNOTES

Introduction

1 Keels, T., *Philadelphia Graveyards and Cemeteries* (Arcadia, 2003).

Chapter 1

1 www.kqed.org/news/10779164/why-are-so-many-dead-people-in-colma-and-so-few-in-san-francisco.
2 "The Town of Colma, Where San Francisco's Dead Live," *The New York Times*, nytimes.com.
3 www.sfgate.com/bayarea/article/Tombstones-from-long-ago-surfacing-on-S-F-beach-3618805.php.
4 Milano, K. W., *Palmer Cemetery and the Historic Burial Grounds of Kensington and Fishtown* (History Press, 2011).

Chapter 2

1 hiddencityphila.org/2020/02/playing-on-hallowed-ground-hidden-cemeteries-and-the-modern-city/.
2 buckscountyhistory.com/cemeteries/Bensalem/lafayette_cemetery.htm.

Chapter 3

1 www.philadelphiabuildings.org/pab/app/image_gallery.cfm/138915.
2 temple-news.com/geasey-tombstones.
3 Stott, A., "Personhood and Agency: A Theoretical Approach to Gravemarkers in Mainstream American Cemeteries," Markers, Vol. XXXV, Association for Gravestone Studies (Sterling Printing, 2019).
4 thecemeterytraveler.blogspot.com/2011/05/how-monument-cemetery-was-destroyed.html.
5 www.valeriemorrison.com/newsletter.html.

Chapter 4

1 www.mtpeacecemeteryassociation.org.
2 thecemeterytraveler.blogspot.com.

3 Stott, A., “Personhood and Agency: A Theoretical Approach to Gravemarkers in Mainstream American Cemeteries,” Markers, Vol. XXXV, Association for Gravestone Studies, (Sterling Printing, 2019).
4 Mosca, A., "Cemetery Bloggers" in *American Cemetery & Cremation* (June 2024).

Chapter 5

1 www.nytimes.com/2019/03/25/science/colonial-cemetery-philadelphia-archaeology.html.
2 www.inquirer.com/news/philadelphia/human-remains-first-baptist-church-philadelphia-20240721.html.
3 www.inquirer.com/news/first-baptist-church-remains-reburied-20240729.html.
4 www.creativephl.org/oacce-projects/her-luxuriant-soil-weccacoe-playground.
5 www.phillyarchaeology.net/research/project-report-index/bethelweccacoe-report-page/.
6 whyy.org/wp-content/uploads/planphilly/assets_7/bethel-burying-ground-report-october-2013.original.pdf.

Chapter 7

1 Giguere, J., *Pleasure Grounds of Death* (University of Michigan Press, 2024).
2 www.darksomecraftmarket.com.

Chapter 8

1 whyy.org/articles/philadelphia-mount-vernon-cemetery-sale.
2 www.zillow.com/homedetails/3301-W-Lehigh-Ave-Philadelphia-PA-19132/377435640_zpid/?msockid=01271be910f5640a25c30f7c1127652e.
3 www.phillyvoice.com/mount-vernon-cemetery-for-sale-zillow-restoration.
4 www.gladwynejewishcemetery.org.

Conclusion

1 Mosca, A. K., *Gardens of Stone: The Cemeteries of New York City from Colonial Times to the Present* (America Through Time, 2016).
2 www.phillyarchaeology.net/paf-activities/burial-places-forum/.
3 www.phillyarchaeology.net/wp-content/gismaps_maps/BurialMapV4/index.html#19/39.95279/-75.15575.
4 Stott, A., “Personhood and Agency: A Theoretical Approach to Gravemarkers in Mainstream American Cemeteries,” Markers, Vol. XXXV, Association for Gravestone Studies (Sterling Printing, 2019).